D1289725

Old Europe

A STUDY OF CONTINUITY, 1000–1800

Old Europe

A STUDY OF CONTINUITY, 1000–1800

Dietrich Gerhard

ACADEMIC PRESS
A Subsidiary of Harcourt Brace Jovanovich, Publishers
New York London Toronto Sydney San Francisco

ACADEMIC PRESS, INC.
111 Fifth Avenue, New York, New York 10003

United Kingdom Edition published by
ACADEMIC PRESS, INC. (LONDON) LTD.
24/28 Oval Road, London NW1 7DX

Library of Congress Cataloging in Publication Data

Gerhard, Dietrich, Date.
  Old Europe.

  (Studies in social discontinuity)
  1. Europe--Civilization. 2. Europe--Social
conditions. I. Title. II. Series.
CB203.G47   940   81-14872
ISBN 0-12-280720-0   AACR2

PRINTED IN THE UNITED STATES OF AMERICA

81 82 83 84   9 8 7 6 5 4 3 2 1

To my daughter, Maria
And her husband, Peter Marzahl

Contents

3

The Crystallization of Old Europe:
The Formative Period

4

Change and Continuity within Old Europe

5

Incipient Emancipation amidst the Persistence of the Old Order

6

Epilogue: Looking Beyond

Preface

The traditional view of the European past has been overly influenced by the national outlook of the nineteenth century and by the assumption that the modern world was a necessary development whose beginnings were evident many centuries earlier. This point of view places undue emphasis on the elements of a power struggle, and especially on a so-called class conflict, which has been read into the centuries of Old Europe.

The purpose of this book is to show that this interpretation of European history is not necessarily correct. The concepts of Middle Ages and Early Modern Times have been abandoned. I have refrained from tracing early indications of "modernity" in institutions and society, as well as from stressing "national" concerns. Corporate organization and regional attachment are presented as the basic traits of Old Europe. Special emphasis is placed on the centuries when these features became paramount and on the primary conditions leading to their adoption (Chapter 3). These fun-

damental features of the old order persisted despite the changes
wrought by the Renaissance and the Reformation, as Chapter 4
shows. After the late seventeenth century, these features weakened
(Chapter 5), and were abandoned in the wake of the French Revolution and the Industrial Revolution (Chapter 6).

This book is not a history in the traditional sense; it presupposes
a knowledge of the main facts of European history. Its aim is to act
as a supplement to that knowledge, and to provide an overview of
the entire epoch of Old Europe.

An index is not included in this volume. Since this work is not
concerned with individual personalities or with special events, I feel
that an index of names and events would be contrary to the purpose
and spirit of this book.

1

Methodological Prolegomena

It is the human mind that, mostly in retrospect, formulates epochs as subdivisions in the continuous flow of history, the life of humanity in time. How else could we be conscious of a past, and how else could we become aware of the character of the present within the stream of history? Yet once a term for an epoch has been formulated and accepted, the term tends to control our thinking about the past in an arbitrary way. There is no better way to express my deep distrust of many of the conventional "periodizations" than to quote three French historians: Bloch, Braudel, and Febvre. Marc Bloch speaks of "wrong labels which eventually deceive us about the contents." Fernand Braudel warns against "ending up by giving the signs authority over their contents." Lucien Febvre contrasts primitives and historians: Primitives believe that by naming a thing they have assumed control of it; once historians accept a name or term, it controls them—they are enslaved by terms.[1]

[1] Marc Bloch, *Apologie pour l'histoire*, 5th ed. (Paris, 1964), ch. IV, sect. 3, "La nomenclature"; Fernand Braudel, in *Annales,* eighth year (Paris, 1953), p. 70; Lucien Febvre, *Pour une histoire à part entière* (Paris, 1962), p. 717.

Since we cannot deal with the past without relating the specific to some period in time, the reader will meet another conventional subdivision, the century. This, too, is a creation of scholars, of the humanists; *centuria* gradually made its way from humanist Latin into the vernacular. Voltaire could still entitle one of his works *Le siècle de Louis XIV,* without identifying the formerly almost limitless term of *saeculum* with an arithmetical *century.* But now we have become captives to this kind of subdivision, to the extent that some scholars shy away from following up a topic beyond the "century" with which they are expected to be concerned according to the titles of their books. The reader is asked to remember that *century,* whenever by necessity used in the following exposition, is only an approximate term.

Ought we not, then, to abstain from thinking of the past by way of epochs? Such an act would deprive us of bringing order into the ceaseless flow of history. Here we have to ask another question: What kind of order?

Historical thinking is determined by two fundamental concepts, evolution and historical individuality. In large measure they are antithetical, much as change and continuity are. They are precisely the categories by which we can comprehend humankind in history; we see life moving between these two poles.

Since the Enlightenment, the Western mind has seen the past primarily as the progenitor of the present; it overemphasizes the evolutionary element in history. The dialectical system, too, whether in its original presentation by Hegel or in its later Marxian formulation, is dominated by the idea that the historical process moves toward us, or even, in a teleological perception, beyond us toward a final goal of history. The idea of progess is only one facet of this general attitude toward the past.

On the other hand, great historical scholars have endeavored to understand the past on its own premises, to see every segment of history within its own setting, as determined by historical time and by a specific geographical space. This constituent element of historical scholarship can be called *historical-mindedness* or *historicism.* The profession prides itself on having developed ever more refined methods of perception and on having explored ever more sources in order to understand past ages within their own context. Though still far from the goal, the profession has indeed made remarkable progress.

One of the great impediments to historical understanding has been the predominance of the genetic approach. It is legitimate to look for the roots of our own institutions and of our own way of life even in the distant past, yet these phenomena must not be seen in isolation. The beginnings of the modern centralized state, the emergence of a competitive state system, the appearance of particular estates such as the bureaucracy or the bourgeoisie—these have been favorite themes of historians. Not infrequently this aproach has been related to the conviction that inferior or inadequate stages have been left behind. What has been won has been stressed, not what has been lost.

The definition of epochs bears witness to this fact. *Absolutism* is a creation of the political liberals of the early nineteenth century. The term *mercantile system,* from which *mercantilism* is derived, was coined by Adam Smith, in his measured but nevertheless negative evaluation. In these cases, as well as in the interpretation of cities and burghers, the emancipationist urge in economics and politics has colored the description of preceding ages.

In a more indirect manner this is true also for the worst terms that have ever found their way into the vocabulary of historians, *Middle Ages* and *medieval*. As Geoffrey Barraclough has stated, "once we have the idea of the Middle Ages in our head, we become its prisoners."[2] The reader will notice that this book deliberately shuns the term. How did the term come into existence? The humanists had spoken of the preceding centuries as the Dark Ages, because of the decline of language and letters, especially Latin. As a term of periodization, *Middle Ages* was invented for reasons of convenience by Hornius and Cellarius in the late seventeenth century. Its general adoption took almost two centuries. Up to the early nineteenth century, the division into ancient and modern history prevailed, having existed alongside the earlier Christian concept of a sequence of world ages and empires, much as the concepts of

[2] Geoffrey Barraclough, *History in a Changing World* (Oxford, 1956), sect. 4, "Medium Aevum," p. 56.

Christendom and Europe coexisted from the fifteenth to the seventeenth century. As late as 1854 the learned stenographer who wrote down Ranke's lectures to King Maximilian of Bavaria entitled them *The Epochs of the Modern Age.*[3] The editor named them *The Epochs of Modern History,* though the lectures encompassed the whole of European history since the end of antiquity. By that time the concept of the Middle Ages had already made considerable headway. It was not in any way related to historical individuality, but philosophers and historians had been anxious to fill it with substance, either negatively, since the Enlightenment, or positively, since the Romantics.

To return to the question asked earlier: Leaving aside such misleading terms, is there another way to bring order into the flow of the European past? This writer believes there is a way, and presenting it is the very reason for this book. Yet first some clarification regarding the categories of historical thinking is essential.

Earlier, this discussion centered on the coexistence of the evolutionary concept and the concept of historical individuality. The latter—the very heart of historical understanding—requires more precise definition.

As the reader will discover, this book is much more concerned with the *what* of an epoch than with its *why.* Causal explanation hardly enters into the following description. Such a treatment is due to my conviction that at best we can only approximately explain the reasons for the changes in attitude and in institutions. Influences can be traced, special favorable conditions can be uncovered, but neither will explain the character of an epoch. Instead the wholeness of an age, its individuality in historical time and in geographical space, has to be described.

Fernand Braudel has endeavored to open up the historical dimension to social scientists, to make them aware that the phenomena they analyze have depth in time. An interesting discussion about the nature of historical time has ensued. It seems to be the consensus of scholars in all countries that historical time is complex. In the words of Theodor Schieder, historical life consists of many layers, each

[3] Leopold von Ranke, *Ueber die Epochen der Neueren Geschichte,* critical edition by Theodor Schieder and H. Berding (Munich, 1971).

having a different pace.[4] I might resume my previous formulation and simply state that the relative strengths of change and of continuity are not the same in these different layers. Though they exist simultaneously, they do not date from the same past. I am not willing to leave it at that and abandon the concept of an all-encompassing entity for understanding a civilization or an epoch, though abandonment would seem to be the result of the emphasis on the multifarious character of life in history. Such resignation has indeed been proposed.

The key term in Braudel's analysis is *la longue durée*. It is precisely this element in his presentation that has been under attack, though he uses it only sparingly and tentatively. He has, for instance, respectfully but unequivocally rejected Otto Brunner's attempt to analyze the structure of institutions and the nature of human relations over a long time span, approximately equal to the time span treated in this book.

Which criteria, then, are used here for establishing an overall comprehensive view of an epoch in historical time and in geographical space?

Institutions are the very backbone of a civilization and hence of any lengthy epoch. They cannot be seen in isolation. Relatively stable material conditions are a prerequisite. A society's attitude toward life corresponds to its institutions. Religion accepts and sanctions this attitude; institutions uphold it. Institutions and ideas have a common origin; they are of one stem. It is impossible to distinguish which of the two preceded the other. As long as institutions maintain their hold, dissenters, heretics, critics, and independents have only a peripheral place within an epoch. Only when these individuals accomplish the breakdown of traditional institutions and, in their turn, establish new ones, will they move into a central position.

All of this discussion leads to the statement that a nominalist, exclusively humanity-centered, causal approach does not suffice to

[4] Fernand Braudel, "Histoire et sciences sociales. La longue durée" and "Sur une conception de l'histoire sociale" (about Otto Brunner), both now in *Ecrits sur l'histoire* (Paris, 1969); Theodor Schieder, "Der geschichtliche Raum und die geschichtliche Zeit," in *Geschichte als Wissenschaft,* 2d ed. (Munich, 1968).

recognize the kind of epoch that is the subject of this book. Only a concept that is "realistic"—in the sense of the scholastics—can do justice to such a topic.

No priority or causal significance is being given to the components of an era, either to material conditions or to ideas. I believe that a description of the whole of institutional features, from family and house via the different estates to institutionalized religion and political administration, can circumscribe the essence of a long-range epoch, without any ideological implications, whether Hegelian or Marxian. What is presented here is a structure whose emergence can be described, not causally explained.

This structure, then, has to be accepted as an entity. To that extent it is postulated as "real" in the scholastic sense, as an idea. Those who lived in such an epoch accepted its fundamental structure. As far as it was criticized, the aim was reform, not overthrow.

A comparison with the United States may be illuminating. Apart from one great conflict—the Civil War—its history is a history of compromise. Such compromise resulted because a common goal, the belief in democracy and the American way of life, was maintained beyond all contests and discord. The United States of the 1980s is in a profound crisis, not least because, to use a contemporary expression, it has lost its sense of identity. Hence the frantic inquiry with regard to its "image": What has happened to the American dream? What is true for civilizations, or in special cases for nations, such as the United States, is true also for epochs in the broad sense in which they are understood in this book; acceptance of the fundamental structure, explicitly or implicitly, is an integral part of their being.

A few words about the concept of Europe must be added. The institutional structure of Europe and the change from Old Europe to Modern Europe constitute the subject of this book. I am fully conscious of the great national variety within Europe, most of all the difference between Mediterranean and northern Europe, but also of what has been called the cultural "slope" from west to east. The topic is Europe *as a whole*, beyond national differentiation. Influences from outside Europe deserve only brief mention within the context of this book. The geographical limits of Europe, however, have to be stated.

Europe in the cultural–institutional sense is not identical with the geographers' Europe. The eastern border of the latter for centuries was the river Don; geographers of the eighteenth century, in the period of the "Westernization" of Russia, extended the limits to the Ural Mountains. The Europe of this book is identical with the area of the Western church; Russia is not included. The structure of Muscovite Russia in almost all its features differs fundamentally from the West. These differences continued to be noticeable even after Russia had been reached by Western influences.

When dealing with Otto Brunner's analysis of Old Europe, which in many respects is similar to my own, Braudel has suspected him of conservative and anti-Russian leanings. It may be pertinent to state that Brunner, or this writer, or others, like Halecki,[5] find corroboration of their own interpretation where it may not be expected. The investigation of the European past has accompanied me through a lifetime. Comparing Europe with Russia has been an integral part of this investigation. Long after beginning my work, I found that a similar, though brief, analysis of the differences between Russia and Europe had been made by someone who can be accused neither of having conservative leanings nor of being exclusively Europe-centered, Leon Trotsky.[6]

As the story unfolds, the reader will realize to what extent a common European consciousness existed through the centuries on which this book is focusing. I believe that common or similar institutions were responsible for common character.

Only recently has the term *Old Europe* been applied to preindustrial and predemocratic Europe. It may derive from Jacob Burckhardt, who uses it occasionally in his correspondence;[7] it is also implied in Tocqueville's analysis of European features prior to the growth of the "absolute" state.

[5] Oscar Halecki, *The Limits and Divisions of European History* (New York, 1950).

[6] Isaac Deutscher, *The Prophet Armed* (Oxford, 1963), pp. 187 ff. (about a 1912 article by Trotsky in *Kievan Thought*).

[7] Letter to Hermann Schauenburg, March 5, 1846; cf. also the quotations from Jacob Burckhardt in Chapter 6 of this volume.

2

Prologue: The Age of the Monasteries and Early Feudalism

EIGHTH TO TENTH CENTURIES

Delimitation of the Period

When we try to analyze the emergence of a European civilization we face two phenomena: the end of the ancient world and the coalescence of Roman and Germanic traditions.

Henri Pirenne has claimed that the ancient world broke up only after the middle of the seventh century, when the Arabs conquered the southern shores of the Mediterranean and for several centuries interrupted its commerce. Whatever corrections have been made of the "Pirenne thesis,"[1] especially on the economic side, the fact remains that the North African provinces of the Roman Empire—in the age of Christian Antiquity culturally and economically among the most productive ones—were lost for good. The Mediterranean world vanished as an entity. For the gradual shift of strength to

[1] A. F. Havighurst, ed., *The Pirenne Thesis* (Boston, 1958).

9

the barbarian world of the north, this event was of paramount importance.

Up to the Rhine and to the Danube and in parts of the British Isles the barbarian gentes, the strongest of which were the Franks, had occupied former Roman provinces. These gentes were a rather late formation. Their migrations had broken up clan and kindred, facilitating fusion with other elements not related by blood.[2]

For a long time special ethnic legislation had existed for the invaders. By the eighth century the fusion of Germanic and Roman components had been effected. And though Christian worship was far from uniform, in the fundamentals of faith the conversion of gentes, formerly Aryan Christians, to Catholicism created a common basis.

In many parts of later Europe the tradition of the gentes now influenced regional institutions and law. These no longer differed according to ethnic origin; they were distinct according to region and eventually also to estate. Strong counterforces were at work against the return of consanguinity as an important element in folk law. Foremost was the Christian church, which prohibited intermarriage between relatives to at least the fifth generation. Earlier traditions were in the process of being incorporated into a structure whose basic features were to be regional and functional.

Such a development presupposes security from external enemies. The period from the eighth century to the tenth, however, was plagued by recurring invasions, even though the primary Arab threat had been met successfully in the mid-eighth century and a century later a large part of Europe had been temporarily organized by Charlemagne. Throughout most of the ninth and tenth centuries the area from the British Isles and from the North Sea coast down to the Mediterranean was recurrently endangered by pillaging expeditions of Arabs, Vikings, and Magyars. It was a troubled period, with no chance for stability. Missionary efforts and conquests, which under Charlemagne had reached the Elbe River, had to be abandoned for about 200 years.

[2] The most substantial study of the gentes—in Anglo-American historiography usually referred to as *tribes*—is Reinhard Wenskus, *Stammesbildung und Verfassung: das Werden der fruehmittelalterlichen Gentes* (Cologne, 1961).

It was not until the latter part of the tenth century that the invasions came to an end. Erstwhile enemies, such as the Normans, who had settled within the Christian confines, and the Magyars, who by then had adopted more sedentary habits, were to become spearheads of emerging Christian Europe. In the next century, the eleventh, the slow advance of the small kingdoms in the north of the Iberian peninsula was to gain momentum, leading to the gradual reconquest of the Spanish lands of the rich Arab civilization. Simultaneously the Normans, as papal vassals now fully integrated, and as such—to use the words of Arnold Toynbee—representatives of the "Western barbarians," wrested Sicily and other islands from the Arabs.

Devices That Led toward Mastery of the Material Conditions of Life

The next period—from the eleventh century to the thirteenth—was a period of consolidation as well as external expansion, and it saw the transfer of institutions to conquered areas. These occurrences were in part due to greater control over the material conditions of life, which was in turn caused by the adoption of certain devices in the eighth to tenth centuries. These centuries had seen a gradual advance in technology, as we would call it nowadays. Not even the constant threat from outside had halted this progress. Yet only after the invasions had ceased could these devices have their effect.

The new devices that were adopted served an almost exclusively agrarian civilization.[3] The Germanic and somewhat later the Slav peoples, who, apart from natives like the Celts, settled the later Europe, both within and outside the former Roman Empire, had long been sedentary prior to their latest migrations. To be accepted, an innovation had to meet their main concerns, cultivation of the soil and warfare. Only in a secondary way might the new devices eventually contribute to the manufacture of other goods and indirectly to the reawakening of commerce.

[3]For the discussion of technological changes I rely largely on Lynn White, Jr., *Medieval Technology and Social Change* (Oxford, 1962).

Not that long-distance trade had been entirely absent in the centuries with which we are concerned in this section. The guilds of itinerant traders who were protected by a special King's Peace were even tighter, their associations closer, than the later corporate groups of merchants. Yet, they were itinerant. Merchants traveled with their goods; they had not yet mastered the art of writing. They had no place from which to direct business; at most they had depots on the coast or at the mouths of rivers, where goods could be collected and possibly exchanged with other merchants. Nor did merchants form a definite estate; especially in seaborne commerce, both nobles and free peasants participated. Commerce had been at the very center of the ancient Mediterranean world. Now it existed at the periphery of society. Even in the tenth century, when commerce in the Mediterranean world revived, it was not a nerve center of society. Here, as in other parts of the former Roman Empire, quite a few of the ancient cities had indeed survived; shrunken in size, they served mainly as centers of ecclesiastical and secular administration. When cities again became consolidated they found themselves in a world that was fundamentally rural, one dominated by the feudal lord.

It was the lords and peasants who benefited most from many of the new devices whose use for centuries to come was the foundation of European civilization, especially those devices that made possible more efficient use of horses. Contact with the nomadic people of the steppe led to the gradual adoption of the stirrup and the horseshoe in Europe. By the eighth century the stirrup became instrumental in the establishment of the mounted troops necessary to military feudalism. In the next centuries charging by way of mounted shock combat troops was adopted. In military expeditions as well as for communication and transportation the horse's endurance was immensely increased by the horseshoe. In an age when horses are rapidly disappearing from sight, it is worth remembering that well into the nineteenth century connections within the wide expanses of the Continent were maintained primarily through the use of the horse. In the tenth century another innovation, no less fundamental than the horseshoe, was adopted: harnessing by way of a collar that rested on the horse's shoulder and could be attached by traces to a wagon. By the twelfth century four-wheeled wagons, drawn by teams of horses, had come into use.

Other inventions, specific to agriculture, had also been introduced. Manorial water mills came into use for the grinding of grain, and from the eighth century onward the use of the heavy plough spread over Europe north of the Loire and far beyond the Rhine. The adoption of the horseshoe and the harness also improved the rural economy, when the stronger horses frequently replaced oxen as draft animals. But the most important of the new implements was the heavy plough. Unlike the scratch plough of the Mediterranean world, which necessitated cross-ploughing and was suitable for lighter soil, the heavy plough cut the earth deeply, following the contours of the land longitudinally, and simultaneously turned the slices of turf. During the next centuries it became more effective when, owing to increased iron production, parts of it were made of iron instead of wood. With the use of draft animals the tendency to cultivate oblong strips of land increased. Wherever the agrarian emancipation was not followed up by the consolidation of holdings, strip farming remained characteristic for the European landscape prior to mechanization, right up to our own time.

Agriculture and Settlement

Modes of cultivation and the distribution of land varied according to geographical diversity and to different traditions of property-holding and inheritance. Nonetheless some basic features can be recognized over wide areas.

Since the time of settlement by nonnomadic people, cultivation had been steadily advancing. In the eighth and ninth centuries clearings were few; they were separated by vast stretches of woodlands and wasteland. The crop yield seems to have been little more than double the seed.

Cooperation, as later practiced in villages, and characterized by the common use of pastures and woodlands for cattle and pigs, may go back to Celtic and early Germanic times. In Carolingian times the manse was recognized as the basic unit of rural society. Surviving only for fiscal purposes, the term *manse* referred to a peasant household with patriarchal traits. It was regarded as the norm, as the cell of rural society. Increasingly it was to exist within the communal setup of the village, which reached its perfection in the next centuries. Eventually strip farming led to the open-field system with its controlled 3 years' crop rotation (winter seed, summer seed, fallow). This development strengthened the communal traits of the economy.

Especially in mountainous and marshy regions where ranching often prevailed, peasant communities and peasant households of an independent nature persisted through the whole course of European history. We also find scattered communities of free peasants within areas in which feudal tenure prevailed. Yet the number of households under manorial lords, which included the great land-holding abbeys, increased, either under pressure from the lords or because of the need for protection. Some of these households were managed by peasants who were personally tied to the lords (i.e., unfree, or "serfs"). The process, which goes back to Gallo-Roman times, was accelerated by the evolution of feudalism, though by no means caused by it. Moreover, pre-Christian Celtic, Germanic, and Slav civilizations had their chieftains. The assumption that some of these civilizations did not include a superior group that gave protection and in turn required services has been disproved.

What, then, was the relationship between the manorial lord and the peasant commune? Instead of thinking of them as opposing forces, we have come to see them as complementary. Following Otto Hintze and Otto Brunner, a combination of authoritative and associative components can indeed be regarded as the outstanding characteristic of European civilization in its different strata.[4] Seen within a wider context, the lord–peasant relationship, though ex-

---

[4]In Otto Hintze's *Gesammelte Abhandlungen,* 3rd ed. (Gottingen, 1970), especially "Typologie der staendischen Verfassungen des Abendlandes," in vol. I; in Otto Brunner's *Neue Wege der Verfassungs-und Sozialgeschichte,* 2nd ed. (Gottingen, 1968), especially "Europaeisches Bauerntum," and his *Land und Herrschaft,* 4th ed. (Vienna, 1959). For the agrarian sector Marc Bloch has come to similar conclusions: see *Les caractères originaux de l'histoire rurale française,* 2nd ed. (Paris, 1964) and his contribution (ch. VI) to the *Cambridge Economic History of Europe,* 2nd ed., vol. I (Cambridge, 1966).

isting outside and below the feudal ladder, shows distinct parallels to the mutual obligations of protection and fidelity in the emerging feudal system. As early as Carolingian times, the custom of the manor, varying locally and regionally, defined these obligations.

Feudalism

Feudalism combined military, judicial–administrative, and economic functions in the hands of a lord. Not all civilizations have passed through such a phase. Feudalism of this scope was a characteristic of European civilization, though parallels can be found in Japanese civilization. With Otto Hintze we can assume that a specific historical constellation is conducive to the development of feudalism and assists in making the transition from clan and kinship to a larger political order.[5] It is the affiliation with an older civilization—such as that of the ancient world, or in the Japanese case that of the Chinese—that accelerates the formation of large territorial units. Feudalism proved to be a useful means for mastering the new task of controlling wider areas and for providing protection. The feudal nobles had at their disposal the essential elements for mounted combat: heavy armor and horses.

Personal followership, later developed into full vassalage, lies at the root of feudal relations. It has been found in early Germanic and Celtic civilization as well as in the patron–client tie in the Roman Empire. Among the Germanic gentes a belief in the charismatic character of noble families persisted through the migrations. The insecurity caused by the migrations and by the later invasions enhanced the value of personal followership. In its turn it became a dissolving element for clan and kindred; the tie between lord and vassal became stronger than the tie of consanguinity.

The outstanding feature in the ritual of homage and fealty is the mutual assurance of protection and fidelity. As early as Carolingian times, the contractual element was the basis of feudalism, though it had not yet spread as widely into the lower echelons of the nobility

[5]Otto Hintze, "Wesen und Verbreitung des Feudalismus," in *Gesammelte Abhandlungen,* 3rd ed., vol. I (Gottingen, 1970).

as it would in the following period. By the tenth century a special estate was emerging. Though it did not have all the features with which the next epoch, the formative age of the Old European order, was to endow it, it radiated into other orbits. Kingship took on a feudal aspect, and feudal concepts entered into the sphere of religion. Praying hands were no longer raised in worship, but folded, as the vassal's folded hands were clasped in homage by the hands of the lord.[6]

An evolution can be traced that indicates a closer relation with the land. At first vassals usually lived at the lord's castle and were fed and clothed by him; later they were given offices, the revenue of which increasingly came from land. Thus from an early stage the tenure of office was related as much to social position and to income as to function. We shall do well to remember this in appraising the meaning of officeholding in later periods of European history. Finally, the endowment with land as "benefice," which became a general practice in Carolingian times, added an economic aspect to the military and administrative–judicial components of feudalism. Thus feudalism attained its full form: Lordship with a dependent peasantry formed the basis of the emerging social–political order. The fief now consisted primarily, if not exclusively, of the landed estate. The end of the evolution was reached when by the eleventh and twelfth centuries the heredity of fiefs became legally established.

In the early centuries the feudal system as defined here remained restricted to the Carolingian realm. Later it was transmitted to England and to southern Italy by the Normans. On the Iberian peninsula, only the lands of the crown of Aragon adopted it. In León–Castile, the participation of all groups of the population in the Reconquista was not conducive to feudalism. The Scandinavian countries were not affected by the feudal system until much later, and only to a limited extent. At the eastern periphery of Europe, Hungary and Poland absorbed feudal influences into the old structure of consanguinity that shaped their settlement.

[6]I am following Marc Bloch's statement in the chapter "Le paradoxe de la vassalité" of *La société féodale* (Paris, 1939; English trans., Chicago, 1961). My analysis of feudalism is primarily based on the work of Marc Bloch, on Heinrich Mitteis, *Lehnrecht und Staatsgewalt* (Weimar, 1933), and on François L. Ganshof, *Qu'est-ce que la féodalité?* (Brussels, 1944; 3d ed., 1957; English trans., 1952).

Kingship

A peasantry, laboriously cultivating the land and gradually making use of more efficient implements, and feudal lords, combining the functions of warfare and of protection and leadership of villagers—within which larger framework did they operate? It was under the double aegis of king and church that this process of settlement took place. Kingship foreshadowed the slow evolution of nationalities; it was the institution under which most of them eventually developed. The church, on the other hand, embodied, at least in thought and purpose, a wider community, the community of Christendom. In practice this community, from the eleventh and twelfth centuries on, was restricted to the clearly defined realm of the Roman church, of Western Christendom.

Kingship retained many traits from pre-Christian, early Germanic times.[7] It had been of sacred character. Some of the gentes regarded the king as a reincarnation of the deity from which the gens had derived. His main task was the administration of law according to custom, and later on according to written law. The Indo-Germanic root for the Latin word *rex* was *reg*, which means "to care for someone, to help." Through all the consecutive periods of European history, jurisdiction remained the main attribute and task of a king. Next to protection by law came protection by arms. In the period of migrations leadership in war was fused with leadership in peace. The duke as leader of war bands and the king who guaranteed justice became one. Kings were celebrated for their heroic deeds, and they were acclaimed as protectors of the people and of the church. Some were made saints: The martyr–king Saint Wenceslaus became the Czech national saint.

The concept of *stirps regia* derived from pre-Christian, Germanic tradition. It meant that a special blessing was inherent in royal

---

[7]An unsurpassed classic work on this subject is Fritz Kern's *Gottesgnadentum und Widerstandsrecht* (Muenster, 1914; 2nd ed., Cologne, 1954; English trans., 1939/1956). See also Marc Bloch, *Les rois thaumaturges* (Paris, 1924), and Percy E. Schramm, *Der Koenig von Frankreich* (Weimar, 1939/1960). In the volume *Das Koenigtum* (*Vortraege und Forshungen*), vol. III, ed. Theodor Mayer (Constance, 1956/1969), Walter Schlesinger's "Das Heerkoenigtum" is of particular importance.

blood. This blessing, of sacred character, was transmitted from generation to generation. It pertained not to the individual but to the family. Therefore election was selection from the *stirps regia*. The quasi-religious character of kingship was corroborated when in the middle of the eighth century the Christian church added anointment to the rites of enthronement. Following the example of Samuel anointing David, the Frankish bishops and a few years later the pope sanctioned the Carolingian dynasty to replace the Merovingians, who had become incapable of ruling. In an age in which the secular and the ecclesiastical spheres were not clearly separated, anointment was regarded as a sacrament. In the eleventh century Pope Gregory VII rejected this interpretation.

Feudalism added new traits to kingship, as did the ecclesiastical sanction. The church considered rulership a vocation from God and made the king's obligation toward God the keystone of the edifice. He had to rule according to the commands of God and the precepts of the church. As head of the feudal pyramid, the king was bound by the basic concept of feudalism, mutual fidelity. In the coronation oath we can trace the interpenetration of ecclesiastical and feudal obligations. In a tightly knit feudal system and in the hands of strong-willed kings, feudalism could give added strength to royal government; this is exactly what happened later, in England. When adopted by royal families, the feudal principle of primogeniture eventually made kingship hereditary in England and in France. Thus it acted as a counterforce against the division of the realm within the royal family, as practiced in Carolingian times. On the other hand, in periods of storm and stress, as during the invasions, and beyond them, the distribution of administrative–judicial power among feudal lords could and did weaken the royal hold on the people, especially when kings were weak persons, such as the late Carolingian and post-Carolingian rulers, particularly in the western half of the former realm of Charlemagne.

Nevertheless the great example of Charlemagne persisted. He had been both a heroic warrior and a king bent on justice and good administration. In order to make his realm truly Christian he had acted in unison with a learned clergy, which in its upper strata had close ties with Rome. Yet an analysis of the organization and functioning of the church in these early centuries will guard us against overestimating the lasting effect of these influences.

The Church

Since the sixth century, the missionary work of the Christian church had extended beyond the confines of the Roman Empire, into areas that had not been reached by the Mediterranean urban civilization. These efforts had emanated principally from monasteries that existed alongside the episcopal organization of the church, though in close interrelation; not a few of the bishops came from the monasteries. In the Mediterranean cities civil administration had deteriorated, leaving the bishop as the most important official. Dioceses were small, and the bishop was often the only priest to officiate, assisted by a presbyter, the later priest. The more Christianity spread into the thinly settled area of the north, the more the organization of the countryside became a task. Diocese and *parochia* ("parish") could no longer be identical. By Carolingian times the parish and the parish priest evolved as the cell of Christendom. They were organized by a reform in which clergy and rulers cooperated. In the mid-eighth century the work of Saint Boniface, following the model of the Anglo-Saxon church, laid the foundation for this development. By legislation, each villager was assigned to a definite parish. Church membership complemented the process of settlement. Next to the village commune and to the lord, the parish priest and the parish church became a main rivet of the rural community.

In these centuries, even prior to the transformation of hamlets into villages, it is easier to follow the increase in parishes than to appraise the actual impact of the priest on village life. Poorly trained in all but the conduct of worship, he had disciplinary functions from the start. A heritage from the early missionary monks was the confession, which in the course of these centuries seems to have passed into the hands of the priest.

The early monasteries of the Iro-Scottish missionaries had been hermitages, and quite a few of the monks had not been definitely attached to one place. They had lived an ascetic life and had spread the Gospel and Christian morals. Many of them had also participated in transmitting the cultural heritage of the Fathers of the church. In the seventh and eighth centuries the early loose way of association was abandoned and the Benedictine rule was adopted. The Frankish authorities, especially Charlemagne and Louis the Pious, made this change general. Another Latin tradition thus entered into the life of the emerging West: disciplined life patterned after the family with the abbot's paternal control as its cornerstone. This left its mark also on the cathedral church, whose clergy from this point on lived in an associative relation with the bishop. By the ninth century cathedral chapters were formed for the administration of the episcopal church, to which schools became attached.

Here we have a village priest ordained by the bishop; an episcopal church in which, under the bishop as the bearer of apostolic succession, the associative element of the cathedral clergy can be discerned; and, finally, monasteries under the direction of an abbot—does this mean that the later strictly organized clerical estate had come into being?

It would be a misinterpretation if we were to regard the Carolingian clergy as a tightly knit, separate entity. In these centuries secular and clerical elements intermingled. Kingship had a sacred character, and landed lordship prevailed, attaining added strength through its feudal functions. The clergy was as much an integral part of the feudal society as theoretically it was an order by itself, with its distant head in Rome only intermittently exerting influence. Synods were presided over by the king, and not a few of them were *concilia mixta* in which secular lords also participated.

The impact of secular government on clerical appointments resulted from the fact that on all levels, right down to the patron of the parish priest, lords endowed the clerics with revenue and land. "The proprietary church" (*Eigenkirche*) is the term used by some German scholars for this relationship.[8] Bishoprics and their chapters

---

[8]The term was coined by Ulrich Stutz in 1895.

as well as abbeys were in the hands of noble families. Bishops and abbots appointed secular officials to exercise jurisdiction over their tenants. Abbeys, with their often widely scattered lands, were the greatest landholders. The bishops themselves took to arms against the threat to the church from pagan invaders.

Which were the characteristic features of religion in this period? In contrast to both Christian antiquity and the period of scholastic theology, doctrinal questions were a central concern of the Carolingian church only when, as in the late period of Charlemagne, rulers and clergy felt called upon to reject Byzantine misinterpretation. This was a Christendom that was neither anxious to elucidate special points of doctrine nor conscious of large-scale ecclesiastical organization. *Ecclesia* ("church") still meant the whole of Christendom, spiritually, or else the local church—usually dedicated to a regional saint who did not have to be canonized in Rome. It did not refer to the institutional church. Similarly, the term *theology*, later a necessary element of the self-consciousness of the institutional church, was rarely used in these centuries, which, relying on the patristic heritage, did not feel called to interpret the faith rationally.

Instead, worship, the center of every religion, retained its dominion. The liturgical celebration of Christ, primarily the recurrent mystery of His sacrifice in the Mass, the ever new participation in the mystery, remained the common bond. The monks elaborated on this task, and schools attached to monasteries were principally devoted to liturgical training.

None of the hymns of this period made a more lasting impact, up to our own time, than the "Veni Creator Spiritus." It was the ascended Christ in heaven and the unity of God–Father, Christ–God, and the Holy Spirit to which the congregation was dedicated in common worship. Christ in Majesty found expression in the art of these early centuries, not Christ–Man; one rarely sees the suffering, crucified Christ. Easter, the festival of Resurrection, became the central holiday of the church year. God-directed, the documents of art and religion of these centuries differ from those of later periods; sculpture, which by its very nature is corporeal, was all but unknown.

In the service a change toward the separation of the clergy from the congregation can be discerned. Toward the end of the Carolingian period the altar was removed from the people, the seats of the choir were placed on either side of the altar; eventually choir and nave became separated. The priest no longer faced the congregation; he was, rather, detached while celebrating Mass. Correspondingly, within the Mass the consecration and the elevation of the Host took on added importance. The elimination of the vernacular paralleled this development.

Again, however, we ought to be careful not to overestimate the immediate significance of these changes. The local priest was presented by the lord to the bishop for consecration; he was a dependent of the feudal society, which, despite special legislation for the clergy, did not clearly distinguish between the secular and the ecclesiastical.

Neither should the centralization of the Roman church in this period be overrated. Nobody will deny the importance of that fundamental event in political and ecclesiastical history, the "alliance" of the papacy and of the Carolingian dynasty. Beyond mutual support, it meant that on the highest level directions from Rome were solicited. Though liturgy within Western Christendom was still far from uniform, the adoption of the Roman liturgy for the Frankish church by Charlemagne is the most striking example of cooperation and the most important step toward uniformity. The Carolingian high clergy at the time of Charlemagne may indeed be regarded as an outpost of Rome. At other times, however, the connection was tenuous. The archbishops, despite their solemn profession of allegiance to Rome, had a semi-independent position. The pallium was sent from Rome; they were not required to go *ad limina apostolorum* (i.e., to Rome), to receive it. As one of the greatest authorities on canon law, Gabriel Le Bras, has phrased it, only in the next period, with the Gregorian reform, did "the Germanic influence take second place, forced back by the Roman tradition."[9]

[9]Gabriel Le Bras, "Les problèmes du temps dans l'histoire du droit canon," in *Revue historique de droit français* (Paris, 1952), p. 500.

Diversity and Unity

In the next period from the eleventh century to the thirteenth, the Catholic church became the greatest force tying emerging Europe together. Did any unity exist prior to the eleventh century?

In the nineteenth century European history was often interpreted merely as leading up to the formation of nationalities and national states. By the very nature of its objective, my analysis leans in the opposite direction. Yet the emphasis I have put on royal and ducal power indicates that in the formation of the political landscape of Europe, even in these early times, loyalty of a limited range, within the feudal system and beyond it, was a constituent element. Once the gentes had settled, kingship created larger units beyond regional attachment. The Frankish kingdom is as much a case in point as is the Anglo-Saxon kingdom in the tenth century. Political allegiance vacillated between immediate lord and community on the one hand and adherence to the king on the other hand. Prior to the tenth century, loyalty to the same king was the only factor that led beyond the gens.

The breakup of the Carolingian Empire was strictly a family matter, a division of territory within the Carolingian family. Yet this breakup produced the first documents whose language foreshadows what later became French and German. "Frankish" remained the designation for the royal family both in the west and in the east; it related to the gens whose kings the Carolingians had been. In the west the Frankish tradition soon became fused with the emerging entity of France. Similarly, after the Carolingian dynasty had become defunct, a kingdom was formed in the east whose royal family was regarded as Frankish. It was composed of several Germanic gentes that retained a common *stirps regia* for a larger whole, the later Germany.

A "national" undercurrent may be discerned in this process. During the eleventh and twelfth centuries, Europe was composed of kingdoms and principalities that formed the nuclei of the later national states. To return to the question asked earlier: Was there any sense of a larger unity transmitted to them?

The empire of Charlemagne had, for the first time, tied the larger part of Italy to the vast transalpine kingdom dominated by the Frankish dynasty. In retrospect it looks like the core of later Europe. It also was the seedbed of early institutional feudalism, which shaped the face of Europe for centuries to come. Did a consciousness of Europe exist around 800?[10]

The imperial title was conferred upon Charlemagne by the pope, who supported the Carolingians as a counterweight against the Roman emperor in the East, the legitimate bearer of the Roman imperial title. Throughout later centuries—until the coming of the Hohenstaufen of the twelfth and thirteenth centuries—the concept of Roman emperor in the West must be seen within the context of rivalry with Byzantium. For Rome it meant an attempt to rally the *Romanitas* under the double leadership of pope and emperor. The Carolingian clergy lined up with the pope in these endeavors. In the Germanic world, *emperor* had a different meaning. It referred to a super-king so to speak, who had been able to take control of several kingdoms. The term can be found in contemporary Anglo-Saxon England and since the tenth century intermittently in Léon in Spain. For Charlemagne, who ruled according to the precepts of the Christian church, it meant above all the *imperium Christianum,* the government of the Christian gentes. Rarely did Charlemagne contrast his empire as Occidental with the Byzantine Empire.

Such terms as *the Occident* and *Europe*—the latter term occasionally appears in Carolingian times—did not have a clearly defined geographical meaning, as they did in later centuries. A consciousness of Europe as a definite entity hardly existed. Even so, it was of fundamental importance that, in the words of a biographer of Saint Boniface,[11] on the eve of the emergence of nationalities an integration through the Christian church had been effected that made the later crystallization of the Occident possible.

---

[10]Denis Hay, *Europe. The Emergence of an Idea* (New York, 1957/1966); for the early period, see especially Juergen Fischer, *Oriens—Occidens—Europa* (Wiesbaden, 1957) and Eugen Rosenstock, in *Das Alter der Kirche,* vol. I (1928), pp. 461 ff.

[11]Theodor Schieffer, *Winfried-Bonifatius und die christliche Grundlegung Europas* (Freiburg, 1954), p. 47.

3

The Crystallization of Old Europe:
The Formative Period
ELEVENTH TO THIRTEENTH CENTURIES

The period from the eleventh century to the thirteenth must be regarded as more formative than any other prior to the Enlightenment and to the period that saw the French Revolution and the Industrial Revolution. An accelerated pace and a dynamic creativity mark this epoch. Great common movements permeated emerging Europe. After a long process of gestation, classical, Christian, and "barbarian"—especially Germanic—elements coalesced, and Mediterranean traditions were fully absorbed into a structure that shaped the whole of the Continent. Out of common movements, institutions developed that were to last through centuries to come. These institutions would mold the attitudes of the different social groups and their relations with one another from this time on.

Material Conditions

Which were the conditions favoring this unique process, a process that strikes the modern-day interpreter as arresting and fascinating?

First of all, by the end of the tenth century Europe was no longer subject to invasion. The lands held by Normans and Magyars had been absorbed into the Christian orbit. Poland and Bohemia had been converted to Christianity, and Scandinavia, too, was on the way to being Christianized. From this point on the continuity of European civilization was assured. In the future, Europe would not be exposed to destructive onslaughts such as those Russia in the centuries of Tartar control, and India during the Moslem invasions, had to undergo. In contrast, the Europeans were to strike out in conquest and reconquest to carry their institutions beyond the confines of the year 1000 and to enlarge the area marked by a common European structure.

Next must be mentioned an improvement in material conditions and an increase in population, both of which must be seen against the background of greater security; they are complementary to the creativity of the epoch, though they by no means explain it.

By this time the horseshoe and the harness were fully operative, making it possible for horses to haul heavy materials over large distances. Stone buildings had been the exception in previous centuries; after the tenth century a change from the use of wood to the use of stone can be observed. From France and northern England to southern Germany, stone churches and stone castles became the rule in the eleventh century. At the same time waterpower was increasingly harnessed to human needs. Improved water mills were used not only for grinding grain but also for the fulling of cloth in textile production. Toward the end of this period windmills, too, spread over the plains of northwestern and central Europe. Within a fundamentally changed human habitat, stone churches, stone castles, water mills, and windmills had become an integral part of the European landscape.

Recently, economic historians have laid a new basis for our understanding of these centuries, especially with respect to two spheres—economy and population. Despite scant statistical evidence, it has been established beyond doubt that this was a period of economic upswing and increasing population. In some regions, population may have almost doubled. The population surplus was absorbed not only by cities and in conquered and colonized territories, but also by internal expansion. In this period land for settlement was cleared on a large scale, even beyond the extent to which later on, in the eighteenth century, rulers carried out land reclamations. Princes, feudal lords, and monasteries shared the task with the peasantry. Most likely in many areas villages—whether independent or under a lord—took the place of former hamlets for the first time. The European countries thus took on the character they were to retain for centuries: densely settled lands dotted with towns and cities, most of which in turn were the centers for numerous villages.

The Peace Movement and
The Movement for Monastic Reform

When we attempt to appraise the movements that abound in this period, we see that two of them are of fundamental significance: the peace movement and the movement for monastic reform. Initiated in the tenth century, both emanated from the feudal–monastic world and both had far-reaching consequences. They strove to eliminate the discrepancy between Christian precepts and the violence left in the wake of the invasions. In the pursuit of this aim they created new forms of organization that shaped Europe's structure from this point on.

From its very beginning the peace movement was all-encompassing; synods proclaimed it. Under the leadership of bishops, regional associations appealed to every segment of the population. They outlawed attacks on churches and monasteries and their lands and on noncombatants.

With the end of the invasions a new phase in European history had begun. A militia had assisted the mounted feudal contingents in fighting the invaders. It never quite disappeared. For centuries the populace was called upon at times to take part in battles, particularly in areas inhabited by a free peasantry. Significantly, however, in this period we meet for the first time with prohibitions against the peasantry bearing arms.[1] Peasants were excluded also from the widely held right to attain legal goals by feud. Warfare and feud—concepts between which no distinction was made—were limited to the arms-bearing segments of the population, primarily the nobility.

The heavily armed feudal cavalry was the main contingent at the disposal of the rulers. The obligation of the nobility to provide feudal contingents to the rulers continued, yet during the next centuries it took on the form of money payments in not a few countries—an indication of the growing importance of a money economy. By the thirteenth century nobles were increasingly commissioned with raising indentured companies. Militant members of the peasantry could join the mercenary soldiery as infantry, armed with bow and arrow, later also with pikes. These contingents took their place as an auxiliary force, eventually becoming the main force. Other members of the lower strata of the population might be temporarily conscripted, to return later to their community and to their nonarmed social status.

Research has shown a close connection between peace associations and the organization of the emerging cities.[2] Many early formations of an urban militia grew out of a peace militia, giving momentum to the associative principles. The individual lords, great or small, were petitioned for help. The principle of protection of the defenseless prepared the way for the feudal warrior's transformation into a knight.

The decisive impetus came from the movement for monastic reform.[3] It had its share in the peace endeavors, yet its aims and effects were more far-reaching. Centered in Cluny, it radiated from

[1] H. Fehr, "Das Waffenrecht der Bauern im Mittelalter," in *Zeitschrift fuer Rechtsgeschichte, Germanistische Abteilung,* vol. 35 (1914) and vol. 38 (1917).

[2] A. Vermeesch, *Essai sur les origines et la signification de la commune dans le nord de la France* (Brussels, 1966).

[3] For the exposition in this and the following sections I am particularly indebted to Carl Erdmann, *Die Entstehung des Kreuzzugsgedankens* (Stuttgart, 1935); English trans. (Princeton, 1978), and to Gerd Tellenbach, *Libertas: Kirche und Weltordnung im Zeitalter des Investiturstreites* (Leipzig, 1936; English trans., London, 1959/New York, 1970).

Burgundy and Lorraine, the heartlands of the Carolingian Empire, into France and Germany and beyond into Spain and Italy. The reformed monasteries, under the guidance of Cluny, restored strict monastic life and became again the centers of liturgical devotion. Their goal was otherworldly, yet abbots and bishops were the advisers of rulers.

The monasteries remained an integral part of feudal society; they had a strong influence on the aristocratic families that founded them or later became associated with them. To fight in the service of the church became a recognized activity of the nobility. War on non-Christians was increasingly regarded as a blessed venture. By the first half of the eleventh century, prior to the Crusades, French knights assumed their share in reconquering Spanish lands from the Arabs. At this time the liturgy of Western Christendom's peripheral members, the kingdoms of northern Spain, was fully integrated into that of the Western church. Its architecture influenced the emerging Romanesque style.

We know that in this period of greater security the number of pilgrimages increased considerably under the impact of the Cluniacensic movement. Their role in strengthening common Christian consciousness is difficult to appraise. The most important of these pilgrimages was, after the tomb of Saint Peter in Rome and Jerusalem, the shrine with the relics of Saint Jacobus, Santiago de Compostela in the northwest corner of Spain.

In this age princely and royal power increasingly asserted itself. National languages matured and, toward the end of the period, found expression in literary masterpieces in the vernacular. The present-day interpreter must not lose sight of the growing diversity of the people of Europe. Yet peace movements and pilgrimages can be regarded as an indication of coalescence—coalescence, however, without central direction. Suddenly, in the middle of the eleventh century, a power emerged that claimed and for a time assumed leadership over Europe—a power that in action and counteraction contributed more to the emerging social–political structure of Europe than any other force. It is time to turn to the Reform Papacy.

The Reform Papacy

What the reforming popes initiated in the middle of the eleventh century has been termed a revolution, a breakthrough, the beginning of a new epoch.

Indeed—what a dramatic change! The reform movement reached the papacy in the 1040s under the guidance and control of Henry III, the holder of the imperial dignity that had been restored almost a century earlier by Otto the Great. The purification of the church and the world was as much Henry's concern as that of his clerical advisers who strove to purify church and world alike. The Cluniacensic and Lorraine reformers were still at work to make the world as a whole Christian; for them the church was not a separate body. Neither the sacred character of kingship nor its independence from clerical control was in doubt. Henry extricated the papacy from being the prey of Roman factions. Yet 30 years later Henry's son, Henry IV, had to do penance at Canossa; his great antagonist, Pope Gregory VII, a successor of the pope whom Henry III had installed, claimed the right to depose kings and emperors.

In the context of this book, this famous conflict must be seen not only as a conflict between *sacerdotium* and *imperium*, but as an outgrowth of the fight for the *libertas ecclesiae*, for the freedom of the church as a corporate body. Even the term *ecclesia* ("church") underwent a change in this period. More and more it was used for the visible body of the organized church. The old indistinct interpenetration of the religious and the secular realm was replaced by the coexistence of a fully organized church and a distinct laity, though the secular groups and offices were rooted in an order stamped by the church.

In the 1050s the Reform Papacy took two decisive steps in the new direction. The election of the pope was entrusted exclusively to the College of Cardinals, which in this period was shaped into a clearly defined body with international membership. At the same time the schism with the Eastern church became definitive. Conflicts between the patriarch of Constantinople and the pope had not been lacking in previous centuries. Yet only now when a uniform liturgy was introduced in the West, including a modified creed, which the patriarch did not accept, did East and West part for good.

These were events of far-reaching consequence. They are an indication that a new spirit was at work in the West, the rational spirit of logical distinction. It had not been absent in previous centuries, yet only now did it become all-pervading. This spirit did not challenge religion, such as happened in a later epoch. The Reform Papacy used rational definition in order to establish the autonomy of the church as a corporate organization independent of all secular influences.

The sacramental function of the priest had never ceased to be recognized as the core of Christian worship. Yet the early attempt of the Carolingian clergy to set itself apart under its own law had not borne lasting fruit. Only now did the clergy become an order that was set totally apart. The stress on celibacy and the fight against simony—the acquisition of clerical office from lay powers mostly by money payments—were main concerns of the Reform Papacy.

In the Investiture conflict the fight for assigning to the church a sphere independent from secular power came to a head. Now the concern with logical definition served to distinguish between the ecclesiastical and secular attributes of bishops and abbots who were in possession of land and power. The church of the Reform Papacy acquired the characteristics of a tightly organized corporate body, independent, universal, and hierarchical, and of a new militancy. The papacy even assumed imperial insignia and incorporated feudal concepts into its relations with secular powers. It became the overlord of the newly settled Normans of southern Italy and made the defense of the church a central concern of Christian knighthood. These steps point to what has been called "an unusually strong desire to set up legal connections and to transform moral into legal ties."[4] This rational–legal spirit is a characteristic of the period by no means limited to the church. Yet the church, as it were, led the way, making use of the refined tools of legal distinction such as were developed in the cathedral schools. This concern with legal

[4] Tellenbach, *Libertas,* p. 186 (American ed., p. 157).

organization had a strong impact on the articulation of secular institutions, though increasingly legally trained laics functioned as princely servants in the place of clerics.

How are we to evaluate this extraordinary phenomenon, the papacy of the reform movement? Its impact on Europe was enormous; its ambiguous character is apparent.

In the spirit of true reform it led the way toward a social–political order penetrated by Christian concepts. More than a century later, at the Fourth Lateran Council of 1215, Pope Innocent III, the greatest of the successors of Gregory VII, gave the sacraments their final definition and limited their number to seven. Henceforth royal consecration was excluded; the sacraments from baptism to extreme unction guided human life from birth to death. The sacerdotal church was strengthened by elaborating on transubstantiation in the Mass, and ordination was declared to give the priest an indelible character. Half a century later Corpus Christi, the festival of the Eucharist, was introduced to glorify the church. Corpus Christi was to become the great holiday which the secular estates, following the clergy in strict hierarchical order, celebrated in solemn procession.

Liberation of the church from secular control was not enough, however. Militant popes attempted to overawe the political powers. In this endeavor the church became as highly organized as any of the secular powers. While striving for rationality and efficiency, both church and secular powers learned from each other. One of the greatest present-day critics in the Catholic church, Joseph A. Jungmann, who has influenced a fundamental reform of the liturgy, has stated that in the following centuries the church became "predominantly an earthly sociological entity."[5] Nevertheless he admits that "the whole economical and political life of the people, society from peasant to king, was framed within a supernatural order." Certainly canon law was already formed in the early Christian church and may have remained, as Adolf von Harnack claimed against Rudolf Sohm, an essential element even in centuries of a disorganized church—of a proprietary church under Germanic influences. Yet only now, in the wake of the Reform Papacy, was

[5] Joseph A. Jungmann, *Pastoral Liturgy* (New York, 1962), pp. 78 ff.

canon law established as a discipline, making its decisive contribution to the transformation of the church into a highly centralized corporate body.

Artistic and Intellectual Development

The transformation of the church, striking and decisive as it was, was part of a change in fundamental, first of all religious, concepts. This change found expression in the art and the thought of the age.

The change in material conditions—denser and more secure settlement and improved transportation of heavy loads—was a prerequisite; yet the new attitude cannot be explained by such conditions. In previous centuries sculpture had been limited to ivory relief carvings, brought to perfection in Byzantine art. The sculpture that made its appearance at this point evolved as a significant mode of expression in Western art. Whatever classical remnants or concepts had a part in the reemergence of the representation of the human body, it was now wholly imbued with the Christian spirit. "The incarnational aspect of the image of man" prevailed—incarnational in the sense that because of the divine Incarnation in Christ the human body was now accepted as a body permeated by the spirit.[6] The image of Christ changed from Christ in Majesty to Christ–Man. Previously representations of the crucified Christ had been rare. Henceforth Christ's sacrifice was the central theme; Christ crucified became the very symbol of Christianity. The Passion was still seen as occurring between the Incarnation and the Resurrection, yet visual representations were concerned above all else with Christ's Passion.

This artistic development was paralleled in the intellectual sphere. Following Charles H. Haskins, the first thorough analyst, the period is usually referred to as the Renaissance of the twelfth century. This movement penetrated the whole of emerging Europe, tying its various countries together much as the church did. To be sure, it had its great chance because of improved conditions, not

[6] Gerhard Ladner, *Ad imaginem dei. The Image of Man in Medieval Art* (Latrobe, Penn., 1965), p. 48.

least the consolidation of cities, to which the burgeoning of institutions of learning is closely related. However, these conditions can explain neither impetus nor direction.

Previous centuries had retained, in the midst of insecurity and disruption, the interest in the legacy of antiquity that had been transmitted by the Latin Fathers. Yet the momentum of the so-called Carolingian Renaissance had died down, and monasteries with large holdings of manuscripts were few. Even so, the importance of these libraries of *scriptoria* should not be underestimated. They preserved Latin texts like Cicero and some of the poets like Vergil, who were to exert a strong influence in the next centuries. Yet rarely had the concern with the Fathers and with the Latin heritage been of an inspiring creative nature. The strength of the earlier centuries did not lie in exposition. Monastic schools had concentrated on training for worship, the very heart of religion. They transmitted to their mostly aristocratic pupils an ever more elaborate and perfected education in liturgy to which the reform movement added momentum.

The logical and legal characteristics of the new outlook are obvious in the endeavors of the Reform Papacy. Yet the movement had a character of its own, reaching beyond the sphere of the church; at times it was even in danger of cutting loose from the matrix of religion altogether. Logic—or *dialectics,* to use the contemporary term—came into its own and soon became the pivotal discipline. In the later twelfth century, and in the thirteenth, associations of teachers or of students—corporate bodies, or *universitates*—acquired autonomy under the protection of the pope or of kings and emperors, a few of them splitting off from cathedral schools. The backbone of their curriculum was the training of the mind, both within the arts faculty and beyond it in the higher disciplines of theology and law.

How are we to interpret the emergence of these institutions, which were to abound in the next centuries? Their exchange of ideas and men surpassed the former network of cathedral schools; they became one of the main intellectual links over wide stretches of Europe, a community of scholars writing in the same language, Latin.

The university must be seen within the wider context of the associative movement of the period. Only very gradually was the generic term *universitas* ("corporation") narrowed down to designate a community of teaching scholars. There was a turbulent period characterized by the presence of migratory teachers; some of them, like Abelard, tried to break away from the cathedral schools. Very soon corporations of teachers or of students were able to establish their own institutions, emancipating themselves—not unlike the cities—from episcopal control. Advisers and administrators trained in the new disciplines, especially in Roman and canon law, were increasingly in demand by both secular and ecclesiastical authorities, most of all by the papacy. It was the papacy that eventually granted to the new institutions the privilege of conferring the *licentia ubique docendi* (a degree that entitled the bearer to teach everywhere). The universal character of the new estate as it is apparent in the scholars' mobility was retained amidst the increasing influence of secular authorities, princely and municipal, on the schools.

The intellectual awakening of the twelfth century opened up a new chapter in the history of Western civilization. Learning and reasoning, henceforth to be transmitted in educational institutions, became an integral part of European civilization. Twentieth-century scholars, including some of the greatest authorities on medieval universities, have been inclined, not just to assign to the movement a distinct character of its own, but rather to set it apart from other tendencies of the age.[7] The thirst for learning, an urge for knowledge per se, has been put forth as the impetus, and the migratory teachers of the early period, together with the wandering students known as the goliard poets, have sometimes been regarded as the first "intellectuals" of the Western tradition. Undoubtedly to the present-day interpreter, who comes from an emancipated intellectual community, these traits appear outstanding. The for-

[7] Herbert Grundmann, *Vom Ursprung der Universitaet im Mittelalter* (Berlin, 1957/1960); Jacques Le Goff, *Les intellectuels au moyen age* (Paris, 1960). On the other hand, the close relation of the universities with the existing social–political structure has been stressed by Maurice Powicke, "The Medieval University in Church and Society," in *Ways of Medieval Life and Thought* (London, 1950).

mative period prior to the full institutionalization of learning has a special attraction for a late-twentieth-century observer. One of the most persuasive contemporary historians, Friedrich Heer, contrasts the "openness" of the twelfth century with the "closed" character of the later period—the period we call Old Europe.[8]

To me, the decisive fact is the very integration of the new learning into the social–political order of emerging Europe. Did this integration take place by necessity, imposed, as it were, by the existing authorities, ecclesiastical and secular? Or was it a continuation of the religious–political tradition of past centuries?

Whatever the cause, the openness of Europe certainly played a part in the further clarification of Christian doctrine and in the intensive absorption of the classical heritage, both of which are major features of this period. Recent research has rediscovered the confrontation with Judaic theology. The central position of the Spain of the Reconquista in transmitting Arabic knowledge has long been known. Through the Arabs, additional writings of antiquity were introduced into Europe. They included a more intimate knowledge of ancient science—mathematics and astronomy as well as optics and mechanics and medicine—but these remained the domain of specialists. Philosophy and theology constituted the core of scholastic training for which the "Latin Aristotle" provided the foundation that also included major writings recovered by the Arabs. Physics thus became related to cosmology, and science to moral philosophy, as indicated by the underlying fundamental concept of the spheres.[9]

The cathedral schools were the seedbed of both method and contents of learning. One of the first schools of medieval humanism was the school of Chartres. It was a master of Chartres who coined the often quoted phrase that, with the knowledge of the ancients as the base, we are like dwarfs standing on the shoulders of giants. Such knowledge was to serve a religious purpose. The thinking of the ancient writers was a manifestation of divine gifts to man. It was to be used within the context of religion, religious striving led the way to

[8] Friedrich Heer, *Aufgang Europas* (Vienna, 1949); *Mittelalter* (Zurich, 1961; English trans. [*The Medieval World*], New York, 1962).

[9] Cf. pp. 112–118, this volume.

it.[10] In the formulation of Anselm of Canterbury, which later scholastics adopted as a directive, *credo ut intelligam* (i.e., only a mind grounded in belief in God can find the way to knowledge). And of the greatest of the masters of scholastic theology, Thomas Aquinas, it is reported that in his last months the "angelic doctor" felt that what had been revealed to him went far beyond anything he had been able to express in his writing.[11]

The structure of the universities bears witness to the basic kinship of faith and learning. As much as learning progressed during the next centuries, and though scholars recurrently even aimed at a philosophy independent of religion, only to be rejected and persecuted by the church, the tie between theology and the other disciplines was never severed institutionally. It is well to remember that into the eighteenth and even the nineteenth centuries divinity remained the most respected of the university disciplines.

The discipline of law, which ranked next to theology, was also a result of the concern of the age with logical distinction. Respect for law, customary as well as written law, had been a fundamental tenet among the European peoples; kings were always regarded as first of all the guarantors of the law. Now the revised Roman law and the systematized canon law began to take their place alongside the older customary and written law. The textbook of canon law, Gratian's *Decretum*, became as important as Peter Lombard's *Sententiae* in theology.

Apart from the theologians, none of the new academic groups acquired greater prestige and greater influence than the jurists. Many canon lawyers who had been involved in the legal and administrative affairs of the papal court became popes. The *doctores utriusque iuris*—the doctors of canon and Roman law—ranked next to the nobility. They were the indispensable supporters and agents of kings and princes and increasingly shaped municipal administration. Romano-canonical law answered the new rational

[10] This is one of the main themes of the works of Wolfram von den Steinen, most of all his *Der Kosmos des Mittelalters,* 2nd ed. (Bern, 1967) to which I am heavily indebted.

[11] Jacques Maritain, *St. Thomas Aquinas*, English trans. (London, 1948), p. 26.

urge, which also manifested itself in the procedural change from trial by ordeal and compurgation—the supporting oath of kin and other "witnesses"—to factual investigation. The learned lawyer and judge replaced a lay tradition that had been based on age-old custom. In most Continental countries the reception of Roman law during the next centuries fulfilled the function that in England was accomplished by the common law. At least as subsidiary law, as *ius commune*, based on scientific distinction, it supplemented the multifarious regional law.

The Cities

Many modern scholars have been inclined to relate the organization of the new schools to the busy life of the cities.[12] The existence of the University of Paris, for instance, is indeed inseparable from the development of the city into the future capital of France. Yet did the cities stand in opposition to the feudal–monastic world? Again we have to ask not so much how they distinguished themselves from older forces but rather how they were integrated into the existing structure.[13]

Nineteenth- and early-twentieth-century historians have tended to weight the interpretation of cities and burghers in favor of "antifeudalism." In the period of the Restoration, Guizot and Augustin Thierry, from whom Karl Marx adopted the concept of class struggle in history, underpinned their fight against nobility and clericalism by equating the burghers of the twelfth century with the Third Estate of the eighteenth century.[14] They did not relate the

[12]Of the numerous books on cities I have consulted, Edith Ennen's masterful *Fruehgeschichte der Europaeischen Stadt* (Bonn, 1953) has been partly corrected in her survey *Die europaeische Stadt der Mittelalters* (Gottingen, 1972; English trans., Amsterdam/New York, 1977).

[13] Otto Brunner, "Buergertum und Feudalwelt in der europaeischen Sozialgeschichte" in Carl Haase, ed., *Die Stadt des Mittelalters*, vol. III (Darmstadt, 1973); D. Gerhard, "The City within the Context of the Old European Order," in *Gessammelte Aufsaetze* (Gottingen, 1977).

[14] D. Gerhard, "Guizot, Augustin Thierry und die Rolle des Tiers Etat in der Franzoesischen Geschichte," in *Historische Zeitschrift*, vol. 190 (1960), reprinted in

sworn communal associations to the associative tendencies of the age. They interpreted the communal movement as a revolutionary force that was by its very nature in conflict with feudal society. Ever since, historians have been tempted by the stereotype of an imaginary "rising middle class," a stereotype only recently discarded.[15] Through research, historians have even reduced to its proper proportion the significance of long-distance commerce in the emergence of cities, which Pirenne and his school investigated with great zeal and thoroughness. Doubtless the merchants' settlement, especially the *vic* ("depot") at the coast or along a river, was frequently the major contributing force for the organization of cities. In colonial territory merchants sometimes were actually the founding fathers of the cities. In most cases, however, cities arose in conjunction with a settlement at the foot of the castle of a great lord or prince, or in connection with a bishop's establishment, in many erstwhile Roman regions out of the remnants of Roman cities. Even the names for the new estate bear witness to this origin: *burgher* (from a fortified place, a *burgh*) or *citizen* and *citoyen* (from *civis via civitas, cité,* "the bishop's see"), names applied to the political members of a city. It was not until the eighteenth century that the meaning of the term *citizen* was enlarged to embrace a whole country. Although many cities owed much to the revival of trade, which they in turn intensified, they must be seen within the context of the agrarian, largely feudal, society. The reclamation of land and the increase in population are as important for the emergence of cities as is the advancement of trade. The splendor and importance of long-distance maritime and overland commerce and of finance should not lead us to neglect the relations between city and countryside. The city had become the market for the surrounding countryside.

The freedom of the city—the special privileges the citizens strove to attain—often had to be won in open conflict with a bishop or

Alte und Neue Welt in vergleichen der Geschichtsbetrachtung (Gottingen, 1962). For Karl Marx's adoption of the term *class struggle* from Augustin Thierry, cf. his letter to Friedrich Engels of July 27, 1854, and his letter to Weydemeyer of March 5, 1852.

[15] J. H. Hexter, "The Myth of the Middle Class in Tudor England," in *Reappraisals in History* (London, 1961).

lord. This does not imply that the cities stood in opposition to the dominant feudal and clerical society, rather, they fought for their place within this society. The *maiores* and *meliores*, prefiguring the later patriciate, existed in most cities from the very beginning of their history. Merchants as well as nobles or other men of note from the entourage of bishops and lords comprised this group.

What distinguished the city was an autonomy guaranteed in charters, whether these were granted voluntarily or gained as a result of conflict. The freedom of the city and the peace it assured for its inhabitants constituted an achievement within the context of the associative movements. The protection the city offered had its special attraction, though it is difficult to trace among its inhabitants the runaway serf, a stereotype of historians. The settlement of the countryside likewise presented improved conditions to the bulk of the rural population. Not a few of the rural communes resembled the cities with regard to the rights granted to persons in them by princes and lords; the Gâtinais, south of Paris, is a case in point.

Burghers of the walled cities did indeed develop a special concept of honor and a kind of pride that distinguished them from the peasantry. These traits resulted to a great extent from the militant character of the city. In Italy, where the city and feudalism were closely integrated, the towers of a town such as San Gimignano still bear witness to the bellicose character of the city nobles. Farther north, too, cities stood their ground in a feudal world; some of them have been likened by French historians of the late nineteenth century to *seigneuries collectives*.[16]

Such militancy paralleled the lordship that the city government exercised at home. Cities developed their own municipal law and their own jurisdiction. To be sure, many immunities within the walls of larger cities were free from municipal jurisdiction; the

---

[16] A. Luchaire, *Les communes françaises* (Paris, 1890/1911); critical discussion by Charles Petit-Dutaillis, *Les communes françaises* (Paris, 1947/1970). The detailed and incisive study by Jacques Heers, *Le clan familial au moyen age* (Paris, 1974), shows the significance of noble familes and the strength of their military establishment within the cities, most of all in Italy, but also in southern France, and in some cases Germany.

bishops as former lords often preserved their rights within special areas. Yet apart from such exemptions municipal courts exercised their jurisdiction over all inhabitants. The city was a well-functioning geographical unit, and in many respects its legislation did indeed point toward the future. Municipal law guaranteed the freedom to move as well as the right to marry and to dispose of one's property freely, including real estate, without the consent of a lord. Only on such a foundation could the merchants, the most dynamic urban group, transact business successfully. Merchants and financiers, the indispensable helpers of rising princely governments, gained in importance and increasingly influenced the economic policy of cities. Yet even in countries where the interpenetration of city patriciate and nobility was not as close as in Italy, the leading citizens who manned the city government, including the merchants whenever they shared in it, accepted the feudal society. They acquired land and often attempted to rise into the nobility.

Neither should the uniform character of the city be overemphasized. Under city law a great diversity existed regarding social groups and quarters within the city walls. Toward the end of this period and in the fourteenth century the bulk of the city population, the craftsmen who were increasingly organized in guilds, attempted through their master craftsmen to gain access to city government. They were not always successful and their gains were not always permanent. Below them a mass of day laborers, servants, and marginal people existed in the larger cities, seaports, and capitals. These inhabitants were not citizens in a legal sense; they owned neither house nor shop and were members of neither craft nor corporation. Besides, the geographical subdivisions of the city were paramount. Except in small towns the actual life of the average citizen was centered around the quarter, which often was also the military subdivision, and the parish.

Despite its independence, the city was closely connected with the feudal and clerical society within which it arose. It could absorb new elements of this society, such as the new institutions of learning and the friars, who only became integrated into the church after a struggle. During the next centuries the new learned professions, especially the juridical doctors who frequently intermarried with patrician families, became a mainstay of city government, which increasingly encroached upon ecclesiastical jurisdiction.

Emancipation from clerical control did not weaken the ties with church and religion. The craft guilds often grew out of religious fraternities; each craft had its own special saint besides the saint of the city. The great Gothic cathedrals to whose construction the cities munificently contributed were major objects of civic pride. No symbol of civic independence was prized more highly by Italian cities than the *carroccio,* the wagon bearing the city's standard into battle. It was here, also, that the cross was made use of in warfare for the first time as the sign of a new militant Christianity, in the eleventh century.[17]

The Countryside

A church that had acquired independence from secular power and set the clergy more distinctly apart from the laity than ever before; a corporately organized learned profession that, though still embedded in the church, developed an honor of its own in separate institutions; cities that engendered a specific municipal pride—all these give evidence of a new phase in European history. As pointed out earlier, greater security and an increase in population were underlying conditions for this change. Fundamentally this change was characterized by a more rational organization of government and law, both within the church and in secular administration, and by the crystallization of "estates." In the words of Marc Bloch, the personal relations, the *lignes verticales* that had prevailed in previous centuries, became less important than the *couches horizontales,* the grouping in social layers in a more densely settled Europe.[18] The "liberty" of the church, of the universities, and of the cities is part

[17] Cf. Carl Erdmann, *Die Entstehung,* and D. Waley, *The Italian City Republics* (New York, 1969), ch. IV. sect. "Patriotism."

[18] Marc Bloch, *Les caractères originaux de l'histoire rurale française* (Paris, 1952), ch. 4, pp. 60–83.

of this new phase, as are the changes that took place among peasantry and nobility.

The process by which villages superseded former hamlets may have stretched over centuries in many areas; now it was accelerated. The village with its close habitation became the rule in regions that were not mountainous or swampy.

In various areas at different times, the old manor began to break up. Cultivation of the fields by the common efforts of both peasantry and manorial lord or his agents became rare. Instead the peasant economy prevailed, with special and varied obligations toward the lord. Marc Bloch calls this process, which according to him was finished in France by the thirteenth century, the most decisive transformation in the life of the *seigneurie*: The lord no longer directed the economy, though he remained military commander and judge, the born protector of his men.[19]

Property rights and obligations in the village were far from homogeneous, yet many former legal distinctions lost their rigidity. Slavery had all but disappeared. Emancipation of the serfs progressed, though in some cases personal lack of freedom in the form of socially derogatory serfdom continued to exist. A peasantry rooted in villages became an essential part of the social–political order. Manorial customs, in later periods often interpreted to the advantage of the lord, remained valid. The lord and the village elders cooperated in the maintenance of order—in jurisdiction and administration. Frequently the lord held certain exclusive economic rights, the wine press, the mill for grinding grain, the oven for baking bread. Lordship and commune in most parts of Europe were complementary, as were magistrate and commune in the cities.

Authoritative and associative elements continued side by side throughout the subsequent course of European history, though in quite a few villages, owing to sale or division of property and of rights, several lords could have claims. Eventually only the privileges of lords were to survive, and many of their duties were assumed by the emerging power of the state.

Geographically the lord's castle was outside the village or on a hill above it, whereas the church was in its very midst. With more in-

---

[19] Bloch, *Les caractères originaux*, p. 105.

tensive settlement and with clearer demarcation of parishes, the parish priest became closely associated with the village. The village elders assembled in the church to transact communal business; they partook in the financial upkeep of the church. The lord had the right to present a priest for consecration by the bishop.

Though in most cases the village lacked the basis of a charter, it was an integral part of the corporate structure of Europe. It was a tightly knit group of householders; they exerted patriarchal control over the family. The individual existed only as a member of the family and of the house.[20] Within this structure the peasants fulfilled the basic function of maintaining by their labor the material basis of life for the whole society.

Knighthood

In this period the old feudal nobility was transformed into a fully recognized estate. Its scope had widened and its structure tightened. Lower strata became incorporated into the feudal relationship, among them formerly unfree dependents of princes and of great lords, like the *ministeriales* (unfree officials of rulers) in the empire. The contractual relationship became more distinct, corresponding to the general concern with legal definition. Advice and service—*consilium* and *auxilium*—were duties as well as rights of the vassal. Within the hierarchical feudal order they imply an associative element in the common action of vassals at the lord's court and in his military service. Since from the king at the apex of the pyramid downward a whole chain of vassals and aftervassals existed, most lords were at

[20]Otto Brunner, "Das ganze Haus und die alteuropaeische Oekonomik," in *Neue Wege der Verfassungs- und Sozialgeschichte,* 2nd ed. (Goettingen, 1968). In contrast to Brunner's and my statement, the interpretation of Alan Mac Farlane, *The Origins of English Individualism* (Oxford, 1978), tries to prove that in a number of English villages as a rule a "land market" existed prior to the sixteenth century, and that the peasant owner had complete control over his property. Mac Farlane gives evidence based on parish records, individual wills, and the like, yet he does not prove that these transactions reached beyond the village and its immediate neighborhood. In my opinion the term *land market* is a modernizing expression; it is not fullly justified by his presentation, which in any case is limited to England.

the same time vassals. Marc Bloch speaks of "a kind of equality in the privilege."[21]

By now the most distinctive feature of this estate was the new concept of knighthood, of chivalry. A new code of conduct was added to the older features of feudalism, the mutual fidelity of lord and vassal and the duties of the warrior. Once more we encounter the far-reaching influence of the Cluniacensic movement. The reforming spirit radiated into secular society, religious and feudal concepts fused, and the idea of a *militia Christiana* emerged. Archaic rites were Christianized. The consecration of arms and the dubbing of the knight replaced the initiation of the young warrior by his father.

The papacy encouraged and directed militancy against heretics and against enemies of the papal see. The great expansionist movement of European knighthood eventually spread out in three directions: the Reconquista, the Crusades, and the German eastern colonization. The common experience of the Crusades, notwithstanding mutual animosity and conflicts, left its mark upon European knighthood. By the early thirteenth century there existed "a unity of knightly and political ideals in which the aristocracy of the greater part of Europe concurred."[22]

It may be characteristic for this development that Romance and German languages retained a twofold terminology for this fighting order, one implying moral concepts (*noble, edeling, adlig*), the other referring to military service (*chevalier, knight, Ritter*). No similar connotation can be found in Russian. Only on the fringes of Europe did terms related to kin remain in use for the nobility (Swedish: *fraelse;* Polish: *szlachta;* Magyar: *nemes*). Important as consanguinity remained for noble families, the concept of nobility as an estate prevailed. This estate could absorb free and unfree elements; like other estates it remained open to new members despite its hereditary character.

Originating in Provence the poetry of courtly love was to become

---

[21] Marc Bloch, *La société féodale,* vol. I (Paris, 1939; English trans., Chicago, 1961), pt. II, bk. 2, ch. 4.

[22] R. W. Southern, *The Making of the Middle Ages* (Oxford, 1953/New Haven, 1961), p.76.

a distinctive feature of chivalry at its height. The woman to whom a knight paid homage was to convey gentility. From this time on the idea of knighthood embraced the concept of gentility, courtesy, *courtoisie*. In the realm of religion a parallel transformation can be observed. The cult of Saint Mary was ancient, yet only now did the veneration of Saint Mary take on the character it was to retain for hundreds of years. No longer was she venerated primarily as the mother of Christ God in heaven; rather, she became the Holy Virgin and eventually the mother of the suffering Christ.

Tournaments now became a means to rein in fighting instincts by formalization and to uphold a concept of specific knightly honor. Much as violence and crudeness persisted in fights and warfare, the ideal of knightly conduct was never lost. Obligations and privileges combined with military duties and rights had always been a feature of feudalism. To go to war for the protection of law remained a dominant trait of the aristocratic code. We have come to regard even the feud, which to moderns appears repellent, as a fight for the defense of legal claims.[23]

The knightly attitude was an addition to the older feudal structure. Landholding, or often, after the breakup of the manor, revenues from landed property or from other feudal rights, remained the material basis of noble families. Landholding involved *potestas*, "jurisdictional and administrative rights and duties." Even though eventually only remnants of lordship were retained, the concept of nobility was not to be separated from the concept of *potestas*.

The Meaning of Estates

We have arrived at a point in this story where it becomes necessary to state what the concept of *estate* means in general and what the limitations and consequences of this concept are.[24]

[23] Otto Brunner, *Land und Herrschaft,* 4th ed. (Vienna, 1959), ch. I.

[24] The "corporate" order has been the special concern of the school of François Olivier-Martin and of Émile Lousse. Lousse has given a major impulse to these studies by way of the two series that he edits, *Standen en Landen* and *Études presentées à la Commission Internationale pour l'Histoire des Assemblées d'Etats.* My association with

The framework of estates—the corporate order, as we may call it—by no means included the whole of the population. Numerous groups had no place in the corporate structure, especially the fluctuating elements, such as casual workers and migrants, in the cities. It has been estimated that at least half the Bohemian city population in the late fourteenth century belonged to this group of dependents. Generally the "poor," which means the dependent, and those without "honor" (*unehrliche Leute,* in the later German terminology) existed at the periphery of the corporate structure or outside of it.[25]

Our understanding of the social–political order of Old Europe as it took shape in these centuries has suffered from the intrusion of concepts that were formulated in the nineteenth century. Neither *class,* which presupposes a society of legal equals, nor *elite*—a term coined by Pareto in the face of an egalitarian society—can help to explain the basic features of earlier centuries. Leadership by the nobility was an accepted fact; the nobility was not a new group, like an elite of the twentieth century. *Class,* from the Latin *classis,* was a term that—whenever it appeared, which was seldom—referred to any kind of classification. The contemporary terms were *status, estate, état,* and *Stand,* or else *ordo* ("order"), though the latter expres-

---

this last group has been very beneficial to me. *Corporate order*—corresponding to the German *Staendisches Wesen*—is probably the best English expression to use to denote the general structure of which the individual estates and communities are parts. It is a rarely used expression, though not uncommon. Sir John Neale, in *The Elizabethan House of Commons,* rev. ed. (London, 1949/1963)—at the beginning of ch. I, "The County"—for instance, speaks of "the corporate reality of the county." Cf. also the Saint-Cloud colloquium of French historians in 1967, published in Paris in 1973 as *Ordres et classes,* ed. D. Roche and C. E. Labrousse. One of their main concerns was to make a distinction between modern and contemporary vocabulary without abandoning the attempt to explain the meaning of the old vocabulary in modern language. See especially the contribution of P. Goubert, "Remarques sur le vocabulaire social de l'ancien régime."

[25] For Bohemia, Fr. Graus in *Historische Zeitschrift,* Sonderheft IV, *Bohemica* (1970), p. 70. Sir Thomas Smith, *De Republica Anglorum,* in a passage taken from his contemporary William Harrison (sixteenth century), states that the "forth and last sort of people," following yeomen and burgesses, "are to be ruled and not to rule other."

sion more frequently denoted the subdivisions of the clergy and its affiliations.

Status, estate, state (état, Stand)—all designate a definite place within the human community under God. In the words of Huizinga, "every one of them is an element in the organism of Creation emanating from the will of God, essential and hierarchical, as venerable as the angelic hierarchy."[26] It took centuries for one of these estates, the estate of the prince, to monopolize the term and acquire a dynamic character.

According to an ancient Indo-European topos, the estates were in turn regarded as part of an order that was divided into three basic groups: *oratores, bellatores* or *defensores,* and *laboratores*—clergy, nobility, and that third group referred to in later times as commoners, or the Third Estate.[27] It is difficult to evaluate the impact on the human mind of such tripartite concepts, which are related both to Aristotle and Plato and to the most central part of the Christian faith, the Trinity. Yet the connection of this topos with the estates is very tenuous. Only very late, in the eighteenth century, was the division of political assemblies into three estates functionally justified as corresponding to the division of society into three estates, such as the German *Lehr-, Wehr-,* and *Naehrstand.*

Estates were innumerable, each having its own value and honor within the European social–political order. They were accepted in their multiplicity as the very backbone of this order. Since the thirteenth century, penitentials for the confession listed them—the clergy, the learned professions, the nobility, and so forth. In later centuries art and poetry, such as the dance of death representations, pictured them in detail and always in hierarchical sequence. Dress regulations bear out the distinctive character of the different estates. The conduct books of the seventeenth and eighteenth centuries are a last outgrowth of this order.

In contrast to the greater fluidity of previous centuries, the posi-

---

[26] J. Huizinga, *The Waning of the Middle Ages* (Leiden/New York, 1924), ch. III, "The Hierarchical Conception of Society."

[27] Cf. the works of Georges Dumézil and the discussion by J. Batany in *Annales,* vol. 18 (1963), pp. 933 ff.; also Jacques Le Goff, "Les trois fonctions indo-européennes," in *Annales,* vol. 34 (1979), pp. 1187 ff.

tion of the Jews at the periphery of, or rather outside, Christian society was now defined.[28] The allocation of a special section in the cities to the Jews—the origin of the ghetto—has to be seen within the context of estates. The appearance of the special Jewish hat has been traced to the twelfth century. The Fourth Lateran Council of 1215, which determined the number of sacraments, also defined the position of the Jews and ordered them to wear a special habit. Protection of the Jews was a *regale,* a royal prerogative. It was, like other *regalia,* sometimes conferred on great nobles and municipalities. Yet the Jews had to exist within a social–political order consolidated under the aegis of the church; hence they were considered an alien element. Significantly, the first violent popular persecution occurred, though, as it seems, against the will of both secular and ecclesiastical authorities, at the time of the First Crusade when the reorganized militant church directed a campaign against its enemies.

The estates were hereditary as well as functional. Attempts that have been made to demonstrate the increasing importance of their functional character are not convincing. From the very beginning function was inextricably connected with the special privilege and with the honor of an estate. A person was born into an estate, whether by virtue of legality, as with the nobility, or by virtue of custom.

Yet the estate was not a closed caste. It was possible, if not easy, to marry into it or to enter it in other ways. To use the terminology of sociologists, neither vertical nor horizontal mobility was lacking. New members joined the estate from inferior ranks, or after losing their position in a higher estate; or they entered it by moving from another region. The estate was able to assimilate new members and to inspire them with its specific tradition. The notion of a corporate entity, *universitas* of which the individual was a part, was strength-

---

[28] Lea Dasberg, *Untersuchungen ueber die Entwertung des Judenstatus im 11. Jahrhundert* (Paris, 1965), shows that "the deterioration" in the status of the Jews was very largely a result of the fight of the Reform Papacy against the royalty whose serfs *(Kammerknechte)* the Jews had been. Yet the special ordinances by which their living conditions were regulated correspond to the general turn toward a corporate order.

ened by the reception of Roman law, in which it was a central concept.

By no means should the corporate order be mixed up with the modern, nationally organized "corporate" order, such as in Fascist Italy. Concepts like chivalry or the honor of scholarship or of a craft, when embodied in estates, did not add to the strength of princely power or of emerging nations. Estates were organized locally, at the most regionally; they contributed greatly to municipal pride and to regional attachment. Here we turn to the nature of princely, and particularly royal, government. It drew the greatest benefit from the concern with legal definition.

Progress and Limitations of Kingship and Emerging Nations

Kingship remained central in the social–political order of Europe. *Res publica*—or *république*—was for centuries to retain the general Aristotelian character of body politic, regardless of the form of government. City governments, such as the Italian city-states, which did not recognize any higher authority, considered themselves to be their own princes, in principle not different from monarchies.

Even after the priestly character of kingship was no longer recognized by the church, the belief in a special blessing of royal blood did not vanish. Kings had to cope with a centrally organized church more than before, with popes who claimed to be superior to every secular power and who now achieved such superiority at times. Eventually, these achievements of the papacy proved to be ambiguous. The existence of a supernationally organized church strengthened the forces bent on limiting royal power; often the papacy and the nobility acted as natural allies, much as in Italy the emerging city-states profited from the conflict between the empire and the papacy. On the other hand, in the long run the corporately organized clergy of a kingdom such as France would take a common stand with the crown against encroachments by the papacy.

While settlement became denser and organization on all levels became legally more consolidated, government aimed at tightening its control. The personal ties of feudalism, with the king at the head of the feudal pyramid, did not vanish. With the feudal system still intact and notwithstanding the autonomy of cities and other estates, kings and princes attempted to strengthen their lordship over kingdom or territory.

Secular government as much as the church profited from the general tendency to rational interpretation and rational organization. The principal exponents of the new learning, the jurists trained in Romano-canonical law, became influential servants of crown, princes, and city governments. Their theory of the superiority of royal power over all other rights strengthened royal claims. The concern of the ruler with the common good (*utilitas publica*) and his responsibility to attend to the country's emergencies (*necessitas*), particularly in matters of defense, though not absent in former centuries, was now corroborated by the formulations of Roman law. The idea of a superpersonal crown, to last beyond the reign of the individual king—"the king's two bodies," in the words of Ernst Kantorowicz[29]—took shape under these Romano-canonical influences.

The extension of royal and princely appointments matched these claims. Both in jurisdiction and finance the services reached down to region and locality. In England, a relatively small kingdom, a combination of royal control and regional share in government was to exist for centuries. The justices of the peace, derived from the regional gentry, were largely trained at the Inns of Court in London. Yet England is an exception, because of its common law. Unlike most other European countries, it gradually developed a national assembly of estates whose members were directly appointed or elected by boroughs and counties. In most Continental countries this interrelation of region and center was lacking. In France no regularly convened and periodically assembled general estates materialized, in part because the delegates lacked authority to make final decisions. In Castile, the Cortes were assembled rarely, especially after the defeat of the Comuneros by Charles V, and they

[29] Ernst H. Kantorowicz, *The King's Two Bodies* (Princeton, 1957).

were composed only of delegates from the cities, often dignitaries ennobled by the crown. Hence the officials of kings or princes determined how strongly the power of the Cortes was exerted and felt.

The king was the highest authority by almost immemorial tradition. His principal responsibility was protection by law and by arms. Yet he had to recognize numerous lawful authorities under him, as in turn had the princes, counts, or others, on whom the crown had conferred special privileges. The great rulers of the thirteenth century were concerned most of all with law and justice. Louis IX (Saint Louis) of France and his advisers aimed at elucidating customary law by reason and equity. His contemporary, Emperor Frederick II, king of Sicily, much as his great Norman predecessors, was famous as a legislator. He codified older legal traditions in a lucid manner. In a characteristic formulation he solemnly defined the role of the emperor as that of both father and son of justice.[30] On account of his strong rational government, modern historians have regarded him as the creator of the first modern state. Yet this "modern" ruler retained many old royal traits, accentuated and transformed by Roman law.

Modern terminology can mislead us when we try to analyze the structure of Old Europe. It took centuries for power to be accepted as an abstract concept. For a long time *pauper,* the opposite of *potens,* often meant "powerless," not "poor." By the same token one of the oldest patrician associations, the Cologne *Richerzeche* of the late twelfth century, bore its name because it was composed of those holding power to judge and to administer (rich merchants were among them); *rich* and *poor* were not mere economic terms.

The diversity of law and the difference of judicial procedure according to estates had to be taken into consideration. Royal jurisdiction could be appealed to, and cases could be drawn to the king's court. Outside of England, law remained multifarious, differing from region to region.

Here we meet with another impediment to the growth of royal power, the strength of regional and municipal feeling and institutions, the core, so to speak, of the corporate order. *Pays* was a term

---

[30] *Ibid.,* ch. IV, sect. 2, "Pater et Filius Iustitiae."

used as much for French regions as for the whole kingdom of France. *Land* in Germany meant the individual region within the empire but distinct from it. Even in the most cohesive kingdom of the West, in relatively small England, for centuries the terms *county* and *country* were interchangeable, the latter referring to the individual county as well as to the whole of the realm. Similarly, the emerging term *nation*, which came first into use at the universities, ought not to be equated with our modern nations. In Italy the love of the fatherland—*amor patriae*—praised by jurists and philosophers as a great heritage from Rome, supported civic pride in one's city.

We should certainly not underestimate the sense of loyalty to the crown, especially not when it came to staving off the contentions of universal powers. *Rex imperator in regno suo* was the position taken by French legists in refuting imperial claims. Religious traditions contributed to the identification of king and country. The cults of Saint Denis, of Saint Jacobus de Compostela, and of Saint Stephen go back to early times, though the royal epithets—the Most Christian King, the Catholic King, the Apostolic King—are of a later vintage. Yet even the reign of one of the most powerful rulers of this period, a man who had broken the power of the papacy, Philip the Fair of France, ended in 1314 in a number of regional revolts. The charters that were granted to numerous French *pays* may be regarded as a prologue to the coming disintegration of France in the Hundred Years' War. They belong to a whole series of contractual agreements all over Europe that limited royal and princely power, such as the Magna Carta in England as early as 1215, and the Golden Bull in Hungary in 1222.

Undoubtedly, an undercurrent of national feeling is discernible. It made itself felt in conflict with foreigners, such as Italians or French versus Germans. Even the Crusades provide testimony for such conflicts, as much as for cooperation. It is difficult to appraise what such animosity meant and how close the tie within the linguistic groups was. Neither can we assess whether the gradual rise of the vernacular to a literary language contributed to national feeling. To the community of clerics that transcended national boundaries, Latin was the common language, whereas within later nations linguistic differences remained very strong for centuries. They persisted even in a country like France[31] where the exalted place of the crown and the early development of learned professions and literature gave the Isle de France a central position also in this respect.

Diversity and Unity

In the end the common bond of the written word may have meant more to the unity of emerging Europe than the attempts of emperors and popes to impose their will, attempts destined to be abortive. In the tenth century Otto the Great had revived the imperial dignity; two centuries later the Hohenstaufen enhanced the imperial claim by incorporating concepts of Roman law. The rulers of the kingdoms, however, did not accept such contention of superiority; the king of France in particular claimed his kingdom to be a continuation of the Roman Empire. Much as the Hohenstaufen tried to provide their vast realm with effective officials and sufficient revenues, in the end they were unable to tie together the wide stretches from the Baltic to Sicily.

To what extent did the recurrent wars between rulers disrupt the unity of Europe? Each contestant in a war claimed that the war was a *bellum iustum,* a war justified by hereditary or feudal claims. The devastations caused by warfare certainly keep us from regarding the European political structure of kingdoms, principalities, municipalities, and estates as peaceful coexistence. Particularly when mercenaries were increasingly used instead of feudal levies, the cruelty and ferocity of warfare became aggravated. On the other hand, warfare was neither ''total'' nor continuous. Although the bulk of the people suffered from it, they did not participate. A name like *Hundred Years' War,* a term by which later historians summarized events, is true only insofar as there had been no respite from

[31] Cf. Charles Perrat in *Revue historique de droit Français et étranger* (1950), p. 574 about the remark of a contemporary jurist in 1539 regarding a royal ordinance about the use of French in judicial business: ''Un Gascon ne saurait entendre le Français.''

recurrent ferocious warfare over a very long period. Most of all, even though the most extended wars changed the power relations between dynasties and states, they did not alter the social–political structure of regions that changed hands. Conquest would leave most institutions of a territory intact, both out of a sense of legal obligation and because of the limitations of power. Most wars had limited aims; they did not destroy the idea that individual kingdoms had their place within the wider European community.

Did the popes succeed in accomplishing the unity of Europe by asserting their superiority? There is no simple answer to this question. I have already indicated that the conflict of the rulers with the papacy eventually gave them added strength when their corporate churches lined up with them. In the fourteenth century the church—itself as "secular" as any secular government—entered a period of decline, initiated, if not by the "Babylonian Captivity" in Avignon, certainly by the schism. Besides, the highly organized church immediately became the seedbed of heresy. In former centuries a loosely organized church had mingled with the world, whereas monasteries had striven to pursue a perfect Christian life of otherworldliness. Heretics had been few. From this time on they were to accompany the existence of the church, questioning and challenging its sacerdotal character. Was the Reform Papacy but a fleeting moment in history, as fleeting as the Crusades, whose territorial acquisitions could not be held and which were of greater benefit to Mediterranean trade and to Italian cities than to the papacy?

Such a view would be shortsighted. The church had changed its character. Rome reached everywhere, ecclesiastical jurisdiction increased, appeals to Rome multiplied. Liturgy had become uniform. Doctrines were ever more subtly analyzed, and a learned profession, steeped in theology, philosophy, and canon law, was devoted to their exposition. Only now can we refer to the church as Latin Christianity. This Latin Christianity was to form the backbone of emerging Europe in language and in thinking.

The word *Europe* appeared rarely.[32] *Christendom* or *Christianity* was

---

[32] Denis Hay, *Europe. The Emergence of an Idea* (New York, 1957/1966).

the term used for the whole, later to be transformed by the humanists into *res publica Christiana*. In its institutions and thinking this Latin Christianity showed a remarkable similarity throughout all the different countries. As Tocqueville observed in 1856: "I believe that it is justified to contend that social, political, administrative, judicial, economic and literary institutions of the European countries resembled each other in the fourteenth century more than even nowadays when the advance of civilization has been concerned with clearing all tracks and with lowering all barriers."[33]

Owing to the common movements we have examined, the estates in the various European countries had a similar outlook and developed similar institutions. Though peasants and common craftsmen remained exclusively rooted in their locality, other estates showed remarkable mobility. Clerics and learned professions knew of no insurmountable national boundaries; their common link was the Latin language. It would be wrong to assume that the rise of the vernacular to a literary language had a divisive effect. Embedded in the same or in closely related traditions, literature, like the great accomplishments of Romanesque and Gothic art, did not bear an exclusively "national" stamp. The great themes and forms were to move from country to country, radiating above all from France to its neighboring countries.

The formative period from the eleventh century to the thirteenth had developed a common civilization that was distinct from the surrounding civilizations to the east and beyond the Mediterranean. That the rising states and nations took shape within this matrix was a decisive fact.

---

[33] Alexis de Tocqueville, *L'ancien régime et la révolution* (Paris, 1856), bk. I ch. IV.

4

Change and Continuity
within Old Europe
FOURTEENTH TO
MID-SEVENTEENTH CENTURIES

The Conditions of Life

When we contend that the basic structure of European institutions and a corresponding attitude toward life could be retained through many centuries, we have first to demonstrate that, despite far-reaching modifications and discoveries, the basic conditions of life did not undergo radical changes.[1]

First and foremost this is true for the size of the European population. The penetrating work of contemporary demographers and economic historians about population and economic crises in these centuries can at best give us approximate figures. In all likelihood,

---

[1] Emmanuel Le Roy Ladurie's inaugural lecture at the Collège de France, "L'histoire immobile," in *Annales*, vol. 20 (1974), confirms for France this conclusion. He relates the stability of the population, which, in the long run persists despite ups and downs, to the recurrent role of wars and diseases. The latter resulted from "l'unification microbienne du monde" in the period from 1300 to 1650; the germs spread from the Orient and also from and into the New World.

the total population of Europe increased only by about one-half in nearly 400 years, between the early fourteenth century and the late seventeenth, whereas between 1700 and 1900 it doubled twice. It is, however, only the great period of upswing that in many areas marks the later fifteenth century and the larger part of the sixteenth that has been compared by some historians with the "population explosion" of the nineteenth century.

Though it is difficult to trace the interrelation between economic recession and changes in population, the impact of decline and upswing should not be underestimated. It is probably on account of the economic and social crises and the resulting revolts that Braudel does not accept Otto Brunner's *horizontalité du temps long*, which is fundamental to this presentation.[2] Yet the enduring structure was not dismantled, neither in most cases were the underlying legal concepts questioned by the rebels who claimed but their traditional rights.[3]

Limitations in population change require explanation. Mortality and fertility have to be considered along with what Gerhard Mackenroth has called *Bevoelkerungsweise* ("mode of procreation"), which includes the prerequisites for marriage and the size of families.[4] Intensive demographic research has confirmed that, in contrast to other civilizations, the "nuclear" family, apparent in the manse of Carolingian times, remained the normal unit in cities as well as in the countryside. On most levels of the population this nuclear family was small, as a result of relatively late marriage—often in the mid twenties—and the high mortality rate of infants. Late marriage and a large percentage of singles are a result of the corporate order. The setting up of a household was a prerequisite for marriage, sometimes enforced by regulations. Since the number of houses, shops, and farms was limited, farmhands and apprentices, sometimes even journeymen, lived in the households of their masters.

At times of population pressure migration to new areas provided an outlet. Such outlets were the New England colonies of the seven-

[2] Cf. p. 5.

[3] Cf. p. 69, including n. 17, this volume.

[4] Gerhard Mackenroth, *Bevoelkerungslehre* (Berlin, 1953), especially pp. 119 ff. and 408 ff.

teenth century, Hungary after the reconquest from the Turks in the late seventeenth century, and Russia in the eighteenth century.

The marginal groups that were not fully integrated into the corporate framework—married journeymen, day laborers, cottagers, and the like—grew in numbers when, with the advance of commercial capitalism, a large labor force was needed. As early as the fourteenth century, the putting-out system—under which textile merchants provided workers with material for production at home—was extended into the countryside. These marginal groups were the most restless element, and they were hardest hit by recessions. Living on the brink of starvation, they were exposed to famine and disease to an extent that is hard to imagine. The interrelation of famine and recurrent epidemics has been proven by research. They were responsible for large-scale reduction of the population, more than the devastating wars that depopulated limited areas.

Even apart from the particularly vulnerable poor, all of the European population was extremely susceptible to epidemics because of the lack of hygiene. Investigations have substantiated the traditional opinion of the disastrous effect of the Black Death in the mid-fourteenth century, when whole villages were deserted. For another period Braudel accepts estimates according to which Venice lost about one-third of its population because of epidemics in the 1570s.[5]

The material side of human life was dominated by cold and hunger. And though the aristocracy in both city and countryside was exempt from hunger, it still suffered from cold and disease like ordinary folk. When Louis XIV died in 1715 he was succeeded by his great-grandson. In his last years his son, two of his grandsons, and other members of his family had perished from smallpox and measles.

The Effects of Inventions

To what extent did the improvements and inventions adopted over this long stretch of centuries modify living conditions? How were they apt to change the outlook of large parts of the population?

[5] Fernand Braudel, *La Méditerranée et le monde méditerranéen à l'époque de Philippe II*, 1st ed. (Paris, 1949), p. 273.

Throughout this whole period, "space devoured the time and effort of men." This is what has been said of the rulers of the sixteenth century.[6] How much strength did Charles V have to expend on unending travels through the confines of his European realm! It took more than a month to bring the fatally ill Richelieu from Lyons to Paris. Though messenger service made progress, it was left to the nineteenth and twentieth centuries to make distances shrink. Even a systematic design of road building between cities, tying them together, did not begin prior to the eighteenth century.[7]

In certain fields of production technological advance was greater than in transportation. Yet as Werner Sombart emphasized a long time ago—and Fernand Braudel has restated this—besides draft animals the major source of energy in almost all countries remained wood and water power. Braudel stresses the ingenuity shown in numerous improvements and inventions even though the economy as a whole remained limited by old practices and lacked elasticity.[8]

By the sixteenth century the improvements made in mining, such as the use of iron hammers and blast furnaces, had accelerated production. The exploitation of European mines contributed significantly to the power of great capitalists, such as the Fugger family. Yet as compared with the ongoing Industrial Revolution of the eighteenth and nineteenth centuries, these changes transformed neither large regions nor society as a whole.

Does this hold true also for the three innovations of the fourteenth and fifteenth centuries that from Sir Francis Bacon to Fernand Braudel have been regarded as decisive—gunpowder, the compass and other nautical instruments, and movable type for printing?

In warfare, first of all, by the fifteenth century, knightly cavalry had ceased to predominate, as a result of improvements in the tactics of infantry and the effectiveness of pikes in formations. For a long time firearms coexisted with older weapons. The famous Spanish *tercios* of the sixteenth century were composed of both pikemen and arquebusiers. From the sixteenth century on, artillery assumed

---

[6] *Ibid.*, p. 310.

[7] Cf. p. 133, n. 49, this volume.

[8] Fernand Braudel, *Civilisation matérielle et capitalisme*, vol. I (Paris, 1967), chs. V and VI.

a commanding position in warfare. Cities in a pivotal strategic location thus needed protection by extended fortification with embankments. Only powerful governments could afford the financial outlay for the fortifications as well as for the artillery. Although princely power made further gains by this development, society was not transformed.

The progress in nautical science opened a new chapter, not only in the history of Europe but for humanity. Whatever the origin of instruments and scientific methods, only at the turn from the fifteenth to the sixteenth century did man venture forward into the unknown open seas, beyond the confines of previous navigation, which had never cut loose completely from the coasts. And though the concept of an immediate "commercial revolution" has been discarded, in the long run the countries along the Atlantic seaboard outdistanced those of the Mediterranean in trade as well as in political power. This shift within Europe was not least due to the new colonial wealth. To a large extent the political history of the next centuries was influenced by the power struggle relating to commerce and colonies.

The great increase in trade, the change in production in some areas, and, most of all, the addition of new colonial lands have led some economic historians and sociologists to regard the sixteenth century as a period of fundamental change in the direction of modernity. They date a "European world-economy" from this period and claim that the emerging states deliberately contributed to a division of production between different areas.[9] Yet increased

[9] An outstanding example of this kind of interpretation of the period is Immanuel Wallerstein, *The Modern World-System: Capitalist Agriculture and the Origins of the European World-Economy in the Sixteenth Century* (New York, 1974). In order to prove his thesis, the author distinguishes between production in the "core states" of Europe and the semiperipheral and peripheral zones, each producing in a different way and with distinctly different labor conditions. He also contends that the emerging state contributed to these distinctions: "the crucial distinguishing factor would be their role in the world-economy [p. 136]." Yet the author cannot prove—nor does he try to prove—that state governments had a clear perception of the role of their countries within such an emerging "world-economy." In some countries, especially in the "peripheral zones" that concentrated on agriculture, such as Poland, it can, on the contrary, be shown that the producers—the nobles who in-

specialized agricultural production in eastern Europe and additional specialization of the manufactures of central and western Europe are only a continuation of older trends; they were not deliberately inaugurated. Moreover, industry did not yet undergo changes in labor conditions similar to those necessitated two centuries later by the technological requirements and the organizational tranformations of the Machine Age and the Industrial Revolution.

The output of the Spanish overseas silver mines led to the much discussed "price revolution" of the late sixteenth century, with its far-reaching economic and social consequences. The impact of the ensuing inflation on the various groups of society, particularly in western Continental Europe, has not yet been fully explored. Neither can we state exactly in which period it affected the different regions. It seems to have been felt especially strongly in those parts of France where nobles depended on feudal dues fixed in definite sums of cash instead of labor.

The structure of institutions and society, however, was left unaltered when the colonizing countries extended their power, even though commercial capitalism thereby gained added incentives. Similarly, the colonization of the New World was primarily a transfer of Mediterranean institutions of long standing, including slavery.

Did the impact of these discoveries on the European mind shatter traditional Christian and classical thinking? To quite a few writers and scholars of the sixteenth century, the world seemed almost unlimited, and the courageous ventures of some of their contemporaries into the unknown heightened their sense of the promise of the age. Eventually, the discoveries led to an appraisal of the nature of European civilization as distinct from other civilizations. Yet this was still far off—the "formidable prise de conscience ethnographique" that, according to Lévi-Strauss, the discovery of the New

---

creased serfdom ("coerced cash-crop labor," in the words of Wallerstein)—did not think in capitalist terms right down to the eighteenth century. Cf. J. Rutkowski, *Le regime agraire en Pologne au 18 c. siècle* (Paris, n.d.), p. 46. Le Roy Ladurie, "L'histoire immobile," p. 680, states that "la production des subsistances s'opère grosso modo selon des normes stables, entre 1300 et 1720, également."

World may have aroused.[10] Only in the later seventeenth century did Europeans become aware of the significance of other civilizations.[11] This late change, at the end of the period being discussed, is indeed, in Paul Hazard's words, part of "la crise de la conscience Européenne"[12] that foreshadows the coming dissolution of Old Europe. Prior to that period the manner of perception had not changed.

Systematic studies of a quantitative nature on the output of books in the centuries following the invention of the printing press are of recent date.[13] Only intensive further research may enable us to approach the problem of a reading public with greater confidence. It is well known what the printed book or pamphlet, often embellished by woodcuts, meant for the spread of the Lutheran Reformation. In the half-century prior to the Reformation, along with the output of humanistic writings for a limited public, the main product of the new printing press had been religious books, including translations of the Bible into the vernacular, as well as the writings of the early mystics. The scope of this output attests to the strength of lay piety as well as to the growth of literacy, which is attributable to the spread of schools in the cities.

With the advance of literacy as a result of the Reformation and of confessional conflicts, the number of educated people increased. Yet, with all necessary reservations, it may be asserted that the existence of a larger number of literate, educated groups did not mean that there was a general reading public. Before the later seventeenth century the mode of communication apparently was to address a limited public made up of such groups as scholars, politically in-

---

[10] Claude Lévi-Strauss, *Anthropologie structurale* (Paris, 1958), p. 26.

[11] J. H. Elliott, *The Old World and the New* (Cambridge, 1970).

[12] Paul Hazard, *La crise de la conscience européenne* (Paris, 1935; English trans. [*The European Mind 1680–1715*], New Haven, 1953)—a book that has substantially contributed to shaping my own interpretation.

[13] Cf. the latest appraisal of publications on printing in *Journal of Modern History*, vol. 50 (1978), pp. 490–493, by Elizabeth L. Eisenstein, who had previously devoted several articles to the question, and her *The Printing Press as an Agent of Change: Communications and Cultural Transformation in Early-Modern Europe* (New York, 1979).

terested officials, and writers—special groups within the corporate order. Literature and modes of expression bore the stamp of an aristocratic society. Erich Auerbach has seen a first merger late in the seventeenth century when *la cour et la ville* formed a combined public in Molière's theater.[14] When the public broadened even more, in the eighteenth century, weeklies began to serve it.

By that time also the academies were looking beyond the world of scientists and scholars. Their very appearance in the course of the seventeenth century meant a break with the past. Through the academies, systematic investigation was conducted for the common good. Secrecy and localism, which had prevailed among the crafts, were now definitely abandoned. This fact, too, was the harbinger of a new epoch in European history.

The Economy and Its Impact on Society

Of the burghers who had found their place in the feudal–ecclesiastical world, the merchants were the most dynamic element. Their effect on the economy—the influence and nature of commerical capitalism—has to be considered in order to evaluate change and continuity in the economy. Neo-Marxian historians are inclined to distinguish a feudal and a capitalistic period; some of them date the beginning of the latter from the fourteenth century.

The influence of commerce made itself felt all over Europe, most of all in the coastal areas, once it had taken on new dimensions during the period of the Crusades and of the eastward expansion. Maritime commerce and the growth of shipping were complementary phenomena. In the end, whole nations, such as the Dutch, would depend primarily on shipping as the cornerstone of their economy; toward the end of this period organized navies grew out of the merchant marine.

To what extent was manufacturing affected by commercial capitalism? Long-distance trade penetrated wide areas, not only from

---

[14] Reprinted in *Vier Untersuchungen zur Geschichte der Franzoesischen Bildung* (Bern, 1951).

the great commercial emporia of Italy, such as Venice or Genoa, which conquered and organized colonial empires. Tuscany and Flanders as well as French and German regions provide striking examples of how long-distance trade based on manufactures radiated into the countryside and established a commercial nexus with large segments of the population.

In previous centuries commerce had dealt largely in luxury goods, many from outside Europe. From this time on consumer goods took their place alongside the luxuries increasingly demanded by the princely courts. The leading manufacture of Europe, the textile industry, catered to both of these demands. More than any other production it became vulnerable to the effects of economic contraction. Many of its workers lived within the city walls; more frequently, under the putting-out system, merchant capitalists distributed work and materials to outlying parts of the city, and to the countryside as well. In both cases the workers lacked communal consciousness and cohesion. They often lived dispersed, rarely in special quarters as the members of the craft guilds did. Nor were large groups of workers fused by their work into a common mold. Where machinery such as iron hammers or fulling mills entered into the production process, the labor force was distributed over many small enterprises.

Under the impact of commercial capitalism a large number of workers were dependent on individual merchants or on companies of merchants, even to the extent that sometimes the output of a whole craft guild depended on the merchant capitalist's demand. The capital, however, remained commercial; it was not invested in means of production to any large extent. Nor did the process of production undergo a change toward centrally directed, strictly disciplined performance. The connection between workers in different localities remained even more tenuous than the rare interurban ties of guilds or journeymen. The local and regional attachment and the dependence on the individual employer were decisive. Thus the groups below the corporate level that existed at the margin of society conformed with the chief characteristic of the social–political structure, its local and regional character.

To what extent did agriculture, which still occupied the overwhelming majority of the population, undergo a notable change because of commercial capitalism?

To begin with, despite the great variety that existed because of differences in geography and regional tradition, basic features in the cultivation of the soil are apparent. The communal character of the village and some connection with a lord persisted in most parts of Europe until the age of emancipation (i.e., the eighteenth and the early nineteenth centuries).

In many areas the investment of commercial capital in agriculture or adaptation to the market economy made a lasting imprint. New foodstuffs, as well as plants producing dyestuffs, made their appearance. Existing cultivation was refined and sometimes tended to monoculture, as in the case of viticulture. Near larger cities, improvements in canal and road building facilitated cultivation for a market. In the late fifteenth century, and in the sixteenth, capitalists as well as governments were involved in reclaiming land from swamp and sea. After periods of depression or devastation the ennobled burghers and officeholders of the cities were the main agents in the reconstruction of the countryside, often bringing about considerable improvements in production, whether they took charge of the cultivation themselves or participated on the basis of sharecropping.

The turn to a market economy, for meat as well as for wool and hide production, led to stock raising on a large scale. Its social effect was detrimental to the peasantry. In England complaints about sheep driving the farmers from the land were to be heard in the fourteenth and sixteenth centuries; to what extent these were exaggerations is hard to say. Less publicized was the same process in southern Italy. In Castile the *mesta,* the association of the great noble sheepowners, made systematic use of grazing lands. Not everywhere did the extension happen at the expense of arable crops. In Italy and in southeastern France the nonfertile areas used by seminomadic ranchers expanded.

Property changes on a large scale in eastern Europe were related to grain production. In contrast to western and central Europe, since the fifteenth century the exploitation of the demesne (manorial land owned by the lord of the manor) by peasant labor became ever more stringent. On the large landholdings in eastern Germany, Poland, and the Baltic countries the peasants were increasingly tied to the soil. The lord's concern for profits from the export of grain and naval stores was a major cause of the debasement of the peasantry, leading to various types of serfdom.

The impact of these changes was restricted to special areas. Technological limitations and social impediments stood in the way of a dynamic change on a large scale. Prior to the advance of scientific agriculture in the later eighteenth century the yield in grain growing remained much the same, despite improvements in crop rotation, especially by the planting of pulses; it rarely rose beyond four times the seed. As late as the middle of the eighteenth century the campaign of the Physiocrats was directed against feudal and communal restrictions and obligations that were encumbering the cultivator. Irrational and unjustified as many of the regulations of the Old Regime were, they were only the last outgrowth—mutilated and distorted, to be sure—of a legal order that for centuries had been at the core of Europe's social-political structure.

The conditions and the ways in which the European peasantry lived must be understood within their own context. In the words of Marc Bloch, we should appreciate the work of our tenacious ancestors who created the grain, invented the plough, and brought about a fertile alliance of field, woodland, and pastures, without closing our eyes to the imperfections of their work—how poor the fields remained and how the population was constantly on the verge of famine.[15]

Not all of the villagers were full members of the village. Often the economic differences also meant social differentiation, increasingly so in the course of time. From early times a major distinction existed between peasants who owned cattle, even horses, and those who depended solely on their own physical labor and that of their family. The further development of the peasantry varied widely according to different traditions of inheritance in the various regions of Europe. Wherever the law or custom of inheritance pro-

---

[15] Marc Bloch, *Les caractères originaux* (Paris,1964), ch. II, "Traits généraux de l'agriculture ancienne," p. 26.

vided for partition of property, the number of small landholdings increased. These cottagers—*Kaetner, Kossaeten, brassiers, manouvriers,* or whatever they were called—were often excluded from the rights of the members of the village commune.

The triad of cropland, pasture, and woodland persisted as the basis of village life with its strong communal traits. After the harvest, the fields, though individually owned, served most of the villagers; in many areas the use of the stubble as pasture for sheep remained one of the most cherished rights, often including the poorer peasantry who strove to have at least some small share in the use of woodlands as a source of fuel and building material. The use of common pastures—sorely needed because of the shortage of fodder—was one of the most disputed issues between lords and villagers. Conservation of the woodlands was a necessity that was fully recognized by governmental authorities in the later centuries of the period. The starting point for the development of professional forestry was the protection of timber, as much as the protection of the nobility's hunting rights.

The communal cohesion of the village was retained legally as well as economically. The village, composed of the owners of farmsteads, functioned as a judicial court at the lowest level, independently or under a lord. In many countries the village commune formed the lowest unit for taxing purposes, and was held jointly responsible for the tax. The forms of tenure were diverse, even within villages; diversity increased as a result of sales and subdivision. Dependence on a lord, or at least the remaining obligations, differed in numerous ways. Landholding conditions and connections with the market also varied. Nevertheless, the village commune continued to function as an entity and its members retained their power within its orbit. Here, too, property and authority were combined; the house and the *potestas* of the master of the house, the head of the "nuclear" family, remained the cell of village life.[16]

Infiltration by commercial capitalism was only one of many far-reaching changes. With the steadily increasing power of govern-

[16] Cf. Otto Brunner, "Das ganze Haus und die alteuropaeische Oekonomik," in *Neue Wege der Verfassungs und Sozialgeschichte,* 2nd ed. (Gottingen, 1968).

ment the lords lost many of the functions that had justified their claims. These transformations notwithstanding, the social–political structure of village life survived.

Nothing is more indicative of the horizon and the goals of the peasantry than the character of peasant revolts, which, in the frequently quoted words of Marc Bloch, were as inseparable from the seigneurial regime as the strike from capitalist big business. Careful investigations of peasant revolts, both of the fourteenth and of the seventeenth centuries, have yielded remarkable results.[17]

There can be no doubt that in town and countryside many of the revolts were the result of tensions stemming from economic depression combined with increased taxes required by the central governments. The interrelations of simultaneous uprisings, however, were tenuous. They spread over wide areas only in times of deep religious emotion, such as the Hussite movement of the early fifteenth century or the great German Peasant War of the Reformation period. A striving for equality as the natural condition of man surfaced in such periods. To a priest in southeast England who was involved in the great revolt of 1381 and who seems to have belonged to the Lollard movement, we owe the often-quoted verses, "When Adam dalf [i.e., dug] and Eve span—where then was the gentleman?" Often the grievances were the result of declining prices or increased taxation; governments and indebted landlords made demands that were rightly regarded as legally not justified. Neither class consciousness nor the idea of a new and better order is discernible, however, with the exception of the religiously influenced move-

---

[17] Michel Mollat and Philippe Wolff, *Ongles bleus: Les révolutions populaires en Europe aux XIV et XVe siècles* (Paris, 1970; English trans., London, 1973); also Roland Mousnier, *Fureurs Paysannes* (Paris, 1967). Rodney Hilton, *Bondmen Made Free* (London, 1973), analyzes the peasant uprising of 1381 in southeastern England in great detail and describes the antinoble character of other contemporary uprisings on the Continent (Flanders, northern France, Catalonia). In the general evaluation I agree with Guy Fourquin's incisive book *Les soulevements populaires au moyen age* (Vendome, 1972; English [*The Anatomy of Popular Rebellion in the Middle Ages*], Amsterdam, 1978). He sums up his interpretation: "It would be wrong to see an anti-nobiliary movement in the 1381 rebellion, despite Ball's famous text against the 'gentleman' and the fact that some lords did suffer in the revolt [English trans., p. 140]."

ments. Most of these revolts were regional; they harked back to the old order, and their demands were strictly traditional. Most striking—and a further proof for the continuity of the old order—is the similarity of causes, demands, and goals throughout centuries. In the seventeenth century the impositions of government became more burdensome, hence seigneurs and other recipients of rural rents feared for their income; at times they even incited the peasantry to revolt.

Although it is essential to point out the limited effect of commercial capitalism on the social–political structure, it is also necessary to emphasize the wide scope and the phenomenal complexity of the mercantile and financial activities of the time, especially those in which the great Italian enterprises of the fourteenth and fifteenth centuries were engaged. Popes and secular rulers depended on their transactions and on their credit. They conducted trade in international bills of exchange on a large scale, without being hampered in any serious way by canonical prohibitions. Investments of individual creditors, by contrast, were placed in familial enterprises, and not on an international scale. Stock exchanges developed on a permanent basis and took to trading in government bonds only after the period under discussion. Even in the seventeenth and eighteenth centuries many small investors preferred regional bonds issued by the estates; for centuries the most popular French government paper was the one for which the Paris municipality acted as guarantor. Trade in shares of the gradually emerging joint stock companies was for a long time restricted. It was centuries before banks and exchanges began to transact business in fully negotiable paper, in the way and on a scale as we know it today.

This further advance presupposed a concentration on quantitative thinking. Only then did businesslike computing become possible. The development of double-entry bookkeeping in Italy in the fifteenth century indicated the moment when quantitative thinking in terms of assets and liabilities became the basis for business accounting. In due course a special role was assigned to capital and eventually a capital account became established. The adoption of the new methods in the north was a slow process. By the later seventeenth century, discounting of bills of exchange, amortization, and accumulation of capital could be figured out exactly; from then on, time, too, was incorporated into a system of quantitative computing. One of the prerequisites for the advance of business methods was the change from Roman to Arabic numerals, which was effected in the late sixteenth century.[18]

Outside the world of business, time and space were still measured for a long time in terms of concrete human experience whose limits were not transcended.[19] The division of the day into equal hours, as we know it, regardless of the length of day and night, was only gradually accepted, in place of the former monastic *horae* (''hours'') which corresponded to the actual length of day and night. The first clocks, in the fourteenth century, marked only the full hours. Prior to the seventeenth century precision clocks and watches hardly existed. By that time systematic scientific investigations were becoming the rule, and a new epoch was ushered in by the common effort of thinkers.

The Tensions of the Fourteenth and Fifteenth Centuries

No period in European history has been subjected to so many diverse interpretations by historians as the fourteenth and fifteenth centuries; no other period seems to lack to the same extent any guiding principle. At its beginning the last of the vigorous and imposing rulers of the preceding period, Philip the Fair of France, brought about the downfall of papal power, which previously had been the unifying force. Ranke wrote of him, ''Durch sein ganzes Dasein weht schon der schneidende Luftzug der Neueren Ge-

---

[18] John U. Nef, *Cultural Foundations of Industrial Civilization* (New York, 1958), ch. I, ''Movements of the Mind c. 1570–c. 1660.'' For this and the following problems see also Lucien Febvre, *Le problème de l'incroyance au 16e siècle* (Paris 1942/1968), pt. II, bk. II, ch. III, ''Les appuis de l'irreligion: Les sciences?''

[19] Robert Mandrou, *Introduction à la France moderne* (Paris, 1961), pt. I, ch. IV, sect. 2, ''L'espace et le temps.''

schichte.''[20] At the turn of the fifteenth and sixteenth centuries, rulers such as Louis XI of France, Henry VII of England, and Ferdinand of Aragon were in control; Francis Bacon referred to them as the Three Magi.[21] The intervening time, almost two centuries, presents no such great political figure. Royal power was in eclipse. Rivalries about succession, conflicts between noble factions, and striving for regional autonomy dominated the scene.

Should we accept the view of most national historians, who regard the period merely as an interlude on the way to political and national consolidation, and even, by way of resistance to papal claims, a kind of prologue to it? We had better take our cue from another observation of Ranke's.[22] Beyond these antipapal tendencies, and independent of them, he saw the associative principle ever more strongly at work and hence he affirmed that the last medieval centuries presented an abundant fullness of life. In his view knighthood and cities reached a further stage, and their strength eventually contributed to the creation of lasting restraints on royal government.

The advance toward more rational administration at the center of government has been carefully investigated. Unquestionably, progress in accounting and greater insight into available resources—the beginnings of a ''budget''—are noticeable, and most officials of government were trained lawyers. And yet the modern interpreter should be warned not to overestimate this development. It took centuries, well into the eighteenth century, for the full professionalization of government service, beyond legal training, to be accomplished.

Neither did the financial basis of government fundamentally change. The taxing power of the crown remained limited. Both the Roman law concept of the common good (*utilitas publica, necessitas patriae*) and the feudal principle of *consilium* and *auxilium* contributed to justifying taxation. Yet for centuries kings and princes were expected to live mainly ''of their own,'' that is, on income derived from demesne and regalia, whose range they attempted to enlarge. The concept of regalia had been largely developed during

---

[20] Leopold Von Ranke, *Franzoesische Geschichte* (Leipzig, 1868), bk. I, ch. III.

[21] At the end of his *History of the Reign of King Henry VII.*

[22] Leopold Von Ranke, *Weltgeschichte* pt. VIII, introduction (''Ueberblick'') to the history of the late thirteenth and the early fourteenth centuries.

the struggle with the papacy; it indicated the special position of the crown, its lordship over the land. The resources of the soil, such as ore and salt, as well as minting rights or customs duties were among them, though the latter two were controversial. When kings or princes attempted to reach the individual by direct taxation, assessment and collection were nevertheless mostly carried out by the communities, which repartitioned the whole amount. The corporate entities were, so to speak, the consignees of the crown.

Beyond their regular revenues, kings and princes depended on the consent of the country. Discerning observers rightly regard it as an astonishing achievement that the king of France since the later fifteenth century had succeeded in levying a regular tax—legally called temporary, the *taille*—without the consent of the estates.

Focusing on the royal or princely government can blind us; we may fail to realize that plurality of authority was built into the social–political structure. Even the customary distinction between France and Germany is misleading. Members of a special estate within the German high nobility succeeded in establishing themselves as teritorial princes; this was the origin of German "particularism," which in the eighteenth and nineteenth centuries became a main obstacle to national unification. Yet in France, too, regional rivalries and attachment to great lords balanced loyalty to the king. Early fifteenth-century France was "more like a loose federation of principalities."[23] The so-called Hundred Years' War between the English and the French crowns, originating in the claim of the English king to the succession to the French throne, has to be seen within this context. It gave the dissenting princely and regional forces a rallying center when this was needed or useful. On the other hand, it could eventually also serve to awaken a potential national feeling, as can be concluded from the story of Jeanne d'Arc. Adopting primogeniture from feudal law and restricting the elective element—in short, the full development of so-called hereditary monarchy, as it was adopted especially in Western Europe—was of dubious advantage; it often led to conflicts about

---

[23] Le Patourel, "King and Princes in Fourteenth Century France," in J. Hale, ed., *Europe in the Late Middle Ages* (Evanston, Ill., 1965), p. x. For the limits of royal power and national feeling, see P. S. Lewis, *Later Medieval France: The Polity* (London/New York, 1968).

succession. Kings and princes frequently weakened the position of their dynasties by establishing principalities for the younger members of the family. The latter often lined up with powerful magnates in control of wide areas, giving their opposition an air of legitimacy. The magnates could thus claim to fight not the crown, but only its temporary holder.

As late as the sixteenth or the early seventeenth century the king had no "monopoly of force"; only very slowly did the emerging entity of the state acquire exclusive military control. The function of the king as supreme administrator of the law and as defender of the country was never contested. Welfare, in addition to security, became a princely concern in the fifteenth century, particularly the control of the food supply. Yet there were no functionaries to discharge such functions.

The king or prince remained symbol and center of the whole, whether of a region—a territory—or of a kingdom. Visual displays of royal power and splendor became ever more numerous and significant, as manifested by the publicity attached to them; royal appearances in a city, funerals, anointments, coronations—all amounted to a kind of royal religion.[24]

The unity of a kingdom was as much a concern of the country as of the prince. Witness the acceptance of the principle of inalienability; witness the emphasis on the entity of "the crown" as distinct from the bodily king. In eastern Europe, an area of elected monarchs, the concept of *corona regni* went further: It underpinned a persistent union between different kingdoms.[25]

Legitimacy of princely rule and of succession remained the backbone of the political order. The unions of countries presupposed it, whether they broke up again like the Scandinavian or the Burgundian realm at the end of this period or whether they persisted through centuries like the Polish–Lithuanian or the Aragonese–Castilian union, or eventually the Hapsburg accumulation of lands. Unions as well as acquisition of territories did not

[24] Bernard Guénée, *L'Occident aux 14e et 15e siècles: Les états* (Paris, 1971), pt. II, ch. I, sect. I, "Information et propaganda."

[25] Manfred Hellmann, ed., *Corona Regni* (Darmstadt, 1961); Karol Gorski, *Communitas, Princeps, Corona Regni* (Warsaw, 1976), ch. 9.

mean a submersion into a larger entity; the rights and privileges of the individual region remained intact. Whenever a ruler violated them, he was suspected of turning from a rightful prince into a tyrant.

Regional and corporate attachment were respected, and grew even stronger. Estates had always been rooted in locality and region; now those estates that wielded power under a prince—the landholding clergy, the nobility, the municipalities, and in a few areas the free peasant communities of marshes or mountain valleys—were organized by him in assemblies of the land. We must not equate the evolution of what historians usually call representative assemblies with national development. The English parliament is an exception, just like the common law and the English feudal monarchy, which even in early times had supervised local government. In general, these assemblies did not meet regularly; they also remained regional affairs. They became the guardians of local and regional rights and privileges, together with the law courts.

These assemblies took shape as an organization for the benefit of the land and of the prince. Most of them lasted through the whole epoch of Old Europe. Some were later to be transformed into modern parliaments. At the same time, the fourteenth and the fifteenth centuries abounded in temporary associations of various kinds, which came about partly because of the weakness of royal authority; they in turn often further weakened it. Associations of cities and associations of nobles existed side by side, especially in Germany, in order to safeguard special rights.

It would be wrong to construct a fundamental opposition of bourgeoisie and nobility, as historians have frequently been inclined to do. The intense rivalries of cities with nobles and princes were not part of a challenge to the aristocratic character of the social–political structure; rather, the cities wanted to have their place in that structure. The same holds true for conflicts within cities. The so-called "guild revolution"—whenever it was permanently successful, which it rarely was—was far from democratic; it aimed at finding a place for master craftsmen in city government.

The cities, their patricians and their legal counselors, the *doctores*, existed within a world of princes and nobles that, even while moving away from the old feudal relationship, retained many of its characteristics. Princes became less mobile, courts took on more distinction; at the same time their attraction for the nobility increased. Tournaments and the many new knightly orders attest to that close connection between rulers and nobility whose cultural impact in the case of Burgundy Huizinga has described. Princely courts, however, cannot be seen in isolation. When the castles of simple knights were no longer safe bulwarks and when the old relationship of lord and village faded, nobles tended to cluster around "the grand" ones, the magnates, as they are usually called. In the connection between lord and vassal, "livery and maintenance" took the place of the fief. This relationship, as well as the captainship over mercenary troops, existed as a way of life for the nobility in most European countries. The armed conflicts of the fifteenth century, such as the Wars of the Roses, and 100 years later the so-called French Civil Wars in the age of confessional struggles, were largely based on rivalry between high nobles who supported different members of the royal family.

The political tensions we have dealt with may be regarded as a natural outcome of the social–political structure of Old Europe. They indicate how closely related lordship and association were, how the one complemented the other. They attest once more to the aristocratic character of the body politic, whether princely or municipal. This structure with its foundation in region and estate was reasserted at the very time when Muscovite Russia moved in the opposite direction, toward autocracy, while expanding into thinly populated areas; in the process, it became a mobile society with no close attachment to region, in contrast to Europe's firmly settled society.[26]

Unlike the Eastern church, the Roman church had become tightly organized when the Reform Papacy established priesthood as an exclusive order. The clergy had become the "First Estate" of the

[26] D. Gerhard, "Regionalismus und Staendisches Wesen als ein Grundthema Europaeischer Geschichte," in *Historische Zeitschrift*, vol. 174 (1952); English trans. in *Essays in Memory of David B. Horn* (London, 1970). The essay compares Europe with Russia and the United States.

corporate structure. Now the hierarchical edifice and control from Rome came increasingly under attack. No other conflict engendered deeper feelings and heavier involvement.

The crisis of the church came into the open with the schism, but the removal of the papacy to Avignon in the wake of the conflict with Philip the Fair had already brought about the loss of the spiritual center of Latin Christendom. The Avignon papacy— referred to as the Babylonian Captivity—completed what the great lawyer popes of the thirteenth century had initiated. The church became an intricately organized hierarchy; the papal court presented a model of administration, taking advantage of all the regulations of canon law in its relations with the laity. In the thicket of organization it became increasingly self-serving and often gave the impression of allotting only a minor role to its spiritual task. Against this development the movements for reform gained momentum, both within and outside the church, while the secular powers defended themselves against papal transgressions. It is our task to appraise the purpose and the strength of these tendencies.

In a period of almost disruptive conflict, the resistance to the fiscal exactions of the papacy and to its judicial and political interference served at times as a unifying force within kingdoms. It contributed, for instance, to the formulation of the liberties of the Gallican church. When, after its final return to Rome in the fifteenth century, the papacy became thoroughly Italianized, a state among Italian states, the grievances against Rome also became a common concern of the German ''nation.''

Yet even the substantial writings of fourteenth-century theorists about the independence of secular power had not aimed at a secularism that we may be inclined to associate with them. In the words of one of the most penetrating interpreters of emerging ''laicist'' thought, Georges de Lagarde, these writings tended instead to integrate the church into the ''state.''[27] They distinguished and separated in order to reabsorb, in the same way in which philosophy was distinguished from theology so that both would work together. Often the strong anticurialism broadened into an-

---

[27] Georges de Lagarde, *La naissance de l'esprit laique,* at the end of vol. II, (Louvain and Paris, 1958).

ticlericalism. "Only when the sea will dry out and when the devil will be lifted to heaven, only then will the layman become a true friend of the cleric," said a contemporary proverb.[28] In the dance of death representations of the fifteenth century, the clergy continued to take precedence over the laity in all its different ranks. Anticlerical remarks and theories must be seen within the context of an intense longing for reform of the church.

Papal centralism, a hierarchy enmeshed in the intricate network of canon law, the uses made of the laity to the advantage of the clergy—these were the direct targets of the reform movement. Within the church it reached its climax in the Conciliar Theory. The councils of the early fifteenth century were successful in overcoming the worst crisis of the church, the schism. They failed in limiting papal power, and anticurialism kept growing throughout the fifteenth century.

Tensions, antipathies, and institutional problems represent only one aspect of religious life. What especially characterized this period was the vigor and breadth of the religious movements. Preaching became a main concern, particularly among the friars. The pulpit took the place of the lectern, which had been located at the rood screen close to the altar. In the late Gothic period the structure of church buildings, too, was to some extent altered. The naves, though still parallel to each other, tended to merge, in the German *Hallenkirchen* as well as in the famous cathedral of Florence; improved acoustics supported the preacher. Should we regard this change as a turn from Mass to sermon, as some modern interpreters have done? The numerous shrines and chapels within the large churches and the superb altarpieces with which donors and municipalities endowed the churches contradict such a view.

The deep religious longing of the age responded to the emotional appeal of great preachers, but it found other genuine expressions. The greatest of the reform popes, Innocent III, had been the last pope to find a place in the church for a new order, for Saint Francis' message of poverty and humility and for his pupils, the wandering friars. The "spiritualist" wing of the order eventually was ex-

---

[28] *Ibid.*, vol. I (1956), p. 168.

cluded; in the wake of the persecution of the Albigensians the Inquisition took shape. Hence in the fourteenth and fifteenth centuries the ever-broadening stream of piety flowed at the periphery of the church, or outside of it. The mystics, increasing in numbers, many of them belonging to the laity, strove for a personal union with Christ, but not primarily through priest administered sacraments. They had to be on their guard to avoid persecution as heretics, though few of them took an open stand against the sacerdotal church. Rather, it was the marks of priestly distinction that were under attack, such as celibacy or the denial of the cup to the laity. When priests or professors like Hus attacked the papacy and the hierarchical edifice, the church struck them down.

Demands for social reform eventually became associated with religious movements, but modern interpretations of these movements as caused by social unrest have been disproved. Heresies had social implications: In the words of Michel Mollat, the autonomy of religion as the main concern of the age must be insisted on: ''Heresy is a break with the belief shared by society and hence it is as much a social as a doctrinal rupture.''[29] The ever wider spread of religious associations such as the Brethren of Common Life and the impact of mystical writings such as the *Imitation of Christ* attest to it as much as printed translations from the Bible.

A brief evaluation of the universities and especially of theological scholarship should round off this discussion of religious movements. The number of universities grew. Institutionally the new universities became more dependent on secular government than on the church. It can hardly be claimed that this made for a freer and more dynamic development, except in Italy where divinity had never played a great part in the life of universities and where the arts faculty was in close contact with the emerging humanistic movement.

Some modern scholars have interpreted the *via moderna*, the nominalistic school and the influence of William of Occam, as an indication of an emerging individualism and rationalism within the philosophical–theological bulwark of the universities, and as such

[29] Mollat and Wolff, *Ongles bleus,* p. 289.

akin to modern scholarship, which is indeed dominated by extreme nominalism.[30] The denial of ideas as realities and their reduction to mere *nomina* of human perception endangered the intimate connection of theology and philosophy, of religion and knowledge. Instead the two existed side by side. Since nominalism refrained from challenging faith it led to a dichotomy, to the *credo quia absurdum* instead of the *credo ut intelligam* of Anselm of Canterbury. God's will appeared as arbitrary, inscrutable, the "otherness." Yet the road from this halfway station did not lead to secularism and skepticism, as we "moderns" might be inclined to expect. Nominalism had its share in the depth of despair in which the young Luther found himself. From there it generated a renewal of religion. Despite many indications of secular trends, the age was an age of faith. How can the movement of humanism and the attitude that we connect with the Renaissance be understood in the face of such an interpretation?

The Renaissance

Perhaps no other term in European history has been as thoroughly investigated as *Renaissance*.[31] Controversies have raged about the extent of the period as well as about the place of the Renaissance within the wider context of European history.

Rebirth (rinascità, renaissance) was an ancient word fraught with religious meaning. In the sixteenth century it also became associated with the notion of a deeper understanding of classical antiquity. It was used for the arts of the period, and later also for the letters.

Renaissance was not used for the whole period until the mid-nineteenth century. It was Michelet who first used the term in this way. This deeply emotional and highly subjective scholar associated the ups and downs of his personal life—the "rebirths" that he ex-

[30] Paul Honigsheim, "Zur Soziologie der mittelalterlichen Scholastik," in *Erinnerungsgabe fuer Max Weber*, vol. II (1923).

[31] Wallace K. Ferguson, *The Renaissance in Historical Thought* (Cambridge, Mass., 1948).

perienced—with his lifework, the monumental *History of France*. In such a personal crisis he interrupted the chronological order of his history and turned to the *History of the French Revolution*. Ten years later, in a new and happy phase of his life, he wrote the volume of the *History of France* that he had previously been unable to tackle. It was published in 1855 with the title *Renaissance*.[32]

Four years later Jacob Burckhardt's *Die Kultur der Renaissance in Italien* was published; it is this work that has determined our concept of the age up to the present day. In temperament, character, and style the two historians differed fundamentally. Yet even if Burckhardt had not stated that for the title of Part IV ("Die Entdeckung der Welt und des Menschen") he had used Michelet's telling formulation, their assessment of their own age shows a striking parallelism. This appraisal of modern times has influenced the evaluation of the Renaissance ever since.

For Michelet the sixteenth century was dominated by "the heroic burst of an immense will," which signified the coming of a new day. The marriage of beauty and truth reconciled art and reason—"voilà la Renaissance."[33] He regarded the discovery of the world and of man himself as the achievement of the age, as a lasting emancipation from medieval fetters. On the other hand, he contrasted the period with his own times, which he saw threatened by an emerging age of collectivism.

A similar attitude toward the Renaissance is even more apparent in Burckhardt and in all those who in consent and dissent have become his successors. The Renaissance is seen in contrast to the civilization of the nineteenth and twentieth centuries, yet its secularism and its rational introspectiveness—"the discovery of the world and of man"—seem to make it a "prototype" of the modern world. An interpretation that had already been initiated by the Enlightenment[34] took deeper root and sharpened the previously rather superficial distinction between a "Middle Age" and a

[32] Lucien Febvre, "Comment Jules Michelet inventa la Renaissance," in *Pour une histoire à part entière* (Paris, 1962).

[33] Jules Michelet, *Histoire de France*, vol. VII, ch. I.

[34] H. Weininger, "The English Origins of the Sociological Interpretation of the Renaissance," in *Journal of the History of Ideas*, vol. II (1954).

"Modern Time," seeing the Renaissance as the introduction to "modernity."

All these points deserve intense scrutiny. It is necessary to describe the character of the period as well as its impact on the next two centuries, up to the late seventeenth century. We shall, however, deliberately abstain from any concern with the Renaissance as a "precursor." Unless an impact through the next centuries can be shown, such a view, in my opinion, is born of hindsight and is an artificial construction. Yet, we should first clarify the extent of the so-called Renaissance, both in space and in time.

Michelet already stretched the term, to cover the "discovery" of Italy by the French around 1500, in the wake of the Italian wars waged by the French crown, to a Renaissance phase in French history. Later scholars tried to distinguish between the Italian and a "northern" Renaissance, especially in France and England. The latter did not emerge until the sixteenth century, in a late period of the Italian Renaissance, or even after its end. Most of the discussion about the character of the period has centered on the Italian Renaissance, from the late fourteenth century on. The first half of the sixteenth century saw some of its greatest achievements, but simultaneously the relative peace and the splendor of Italy came to an end, destroyed by the Italian campaigns of the newly emerging French, Spanish, and Hapsburg dynastic powers. Hence the Italian Renaissance is largely contemporary with the period analyzed in the previous section. The increased participation of the laity in religious movements and in intellectual life, the importance of association, the desire for religious reform and renovation, and, most of all, municipal pride—these are an integral part of the period, specifically in Italy.

"I merely maintain that the so-called Renaissance period had a distinctive physiognomy of its own, and that the inability of historians to find a simple and satisfactory definition for it does not entitle us to doubt its existence."[35] To this statement of Paul

[35] Paul Kristeller, *Renaissance Thought* (New York, 1955/1961), ch. I, "The Humanist Movement," p. 4.

Kristeller may be added that quite a few contemporaries, especially humanists, were convinced of the promise and the newness of the age. The reference to previous centuries as Dark Ages is another expression of the heightened dynamic self-consciousness of the time, though it was limited to the literary area, especially in relation to antiquity with whose renewed understanding the notion of rebirth became associated. Alongside the traditional Christian view of history, which centered on the Incarnation and regarded empire and kingdoms as a continuation of the Roman Empire, a distinction emerged between "ancient" and "modern" that emphasized the Fall of Rome.[36] To us these two concepts seem contradictory. It is characteristic that they coexisted well into the late seventeenth century. It shows that no fundamental break occurred.

The notion of rebirth can be traced only in the fields of art and literature. Contemporaries contrasted these attainments with past centuries. Of the discoveries of the Renaissance period, painting with a three-dimensional effect—the mastering of perspective—remained basic until the beginning of the twentieth century. The accomplishments in the visual arts have endowed the Italian culture of the Renaissance, most of all of Florence, with a splendor that has caused critics from Voltaire to Burckhardt to rank it and Athens as the two highlights of Western civilization. And indeed, art from this time on became a value in its own right; an independent current was set in motion. Burckhardt interpreted the artistic development as a result of a deeper understanding of antiquity, yet at the same time as a manifestation of the Italian genius. Owing to the humanists, a similar convergence can be seen in the literary Renaissance.

In Italy, rhetoric had been independent of the philosophical–theological analysis to which the training of the mind had been limited elsewhere. Rhetoric stood in the center of the intensified study of antiquity. Yet much as the orator was treasured, he was not esteemed independent of goal and contents. Style had to contribute to the cultivation of the will. To write and to speak well, like the an-

---

[36] Walther Rehm, *Der Untergang Roms im abendlaendischen Denken* (Leipzig, Darmstadt, 1930/1966).

cients, to be inspired by them—this became a distinctive characteristic of the period. Did this mean a break with the past?

The humanists' frequently derogatory attitude toward the scholastics should not mislead us. They did not aim to replace dialectics, though the philosophy of the schools lacked creativity. Their lasting influence, in literature and in education as well as in some fields of science, especially anatomy, added new scope to the intellectual heritage transmitted under the guidance of the church in previous centuries. Latin and, to a limited extent, Greek authors were studied in their own right. Ancient history and ancient life became an independent source of knowledge and inspiration for all those who participated in the cultural life of the West. In the words of Burckhardt, the civilization of all later generations was based on this elevation of antiquity.[37] Until the turn from the seventeenth to the eighteenth century, though, the curricula of schools and universities were to offer a combination of scholastic and humanist studies, of intellectual and linguistic training under the old predominance of religion and logic. Within this framework the Aristotelian component should not be underestimated. Even in Protestant Germany Aristotle, so thoroughly disliked by Luther, was retained through the efforts of Melanchthon.

As to language, humanistic influence went in two directions. At a time when the languages of the nations increasingly asserted themselves, humanism added strength to the tradition of Latin. Among scholars Latin was the preferred mode of communication well into the seventeenth century. On the other hand, the special care given to language and rhetoric had its effect on the vernacular, leading especially to a refinement of the literatures in the Romance languages. Norms and contents of classical literature became an integral part in the development of national literatures. Older traits of a common European culture as well as the emerging national consciousness were thus strengthened.

In the opinion of this writer, the normative element permeates, in one way or another, all Renaissance thinking. Normative images of

[37] Jacob Burckhardt, *Die Kultur der Renaissance in Italien* (Basel, 1866), sect. III, ch. I.

the remote national past, similar to the idealization of the Roman Republic, were created. The wise lawgiver now often holds a central position in legal–political thought; he remains a mythical figure, representing the purpose for which the community lives. *Patria*, the city-state, takes its place alongside Christendom, to some extent overshadowing it. Whatever may have existed of a non-Christian, "pagan" attitude and faith, or of a simple secularism was never conceived as a system and was never used as an aggressive weapon. The cross-fertilization of Christian religion with humanism and Renaissance art is well known. It is apparent in biblical humanism and, to quote Burckhardt once more, in "that one strong stream of veneration of religion and of glorification of the sacred" in Renaissance art.[38] Arguments from antiquity stood side by side with Christian precepts, and Platonic philosophy was interpreted as being in harmony with Christianity. Research on Savonarola has shown that he belonged to a familiar Florentine tradition that regarded the city as both the New Rome and the New Jerusalem.[39] Where civic virtue in the Roman sense became the norm, the incorporation of a dynamic *virtù* into Christian ethics was not excluded, even if we find it difficult to reconcile the two. In one of his most illuminating chapters, on religion and the Renaissance mind, Burckhardt emphasizes the subjectivity of Renaissance religion and the strength of secularism, in contrast to northern Europe where religion remained an objective force *(ein objektiv Gegebenes)*. Nevertheless he refers to the cultured Italians as *religoes geboren*. We should keep this in mind whenever we are tempted to overstress those Renaissance traits that remind us of the attitude of the "modern" world.

The subjectivist attitudes and individualism of the Renaissance should not be seen in isolation. Neither should the mobility of its society be overemphasized. The early scholars of the twelfth century had found their place within the framework of schools, which became an integral part of the hierarchical–aristocratic society. Artists, writers, and thinkers of the Renaissance might be less fettered by guilds and corporate organizations, yet they continued to operate

---

[38] Letter of 1889 to Ludwig Pastor.
[39] Donald Weinstein, *Savonarola and Florence* (Princeton, 1970).

within a social–political structure that had taken shape centuries earlier. Research such as that of Gene Brucker and of Lauro Martines on Florence shows the significance of family, rank, and hierarchy, to which the individual remained attached, at least in a client–patron relationship.[40] Occasional criticism of the hereditary nobility by humanists notwithstanding, the attempts of historians to associate the Renaissance with a bourgeois spirit, in which merit replaced status, are misleading. Much as Leon Battista Alberti, for instance, appreciated success in business, his rational calculation remained within the framework of home and patriarchal family.

One aspect of Renaissance thought and life still requires special consideration, since its "modernity" plays a prominent role in the evaluation of the period as initiating modern times: the autonomy of politics. Burckhardt entitled his first chapter "The State as a Work of Art," in this way underlining the rational and man-made features in the fabric of Italian republics and principalities—features that apparently set them in sharp contrast to the traditional social–political structure of Old Europe. Besides, Florence gave birth to a sequence of historical–political writers and thinkers who are regarded as the first penetrating analysts of the body politic.[41] And do we not find in Machiavelli a view of man who is challenged by the flux of history and responds by ever new decisions—an attitude that today seems akin to the existentialist challenge in what may be termed the post-modern world?

Undoubtedly, empirical analysis entered into the concern with politics as never before, yet we have to be on our guard not to draw too far-reaching conclusions from this observation. It was the specific Italian background—in Burckhardt's words, Italy's temporary "violent and lawless conditions"[42]—that led to the rational study of

---

[40] Gene A. Brucker, *The Civic World of Renaissance Florence* (Princeton, 1977). The very penetrating and substantial book of Renaissance scholar Lauro Martines, *Power and Imagination, City-States in Renaissance Italy* (New York, 1979), shows the oligarchic character of Renaissance culture.

[41] Felix Gilbert, *Machiavelli and Guicciardini* (Princeton, 1965).

[42] Burckhardt, *Die Kultur,* sect. VI, ch. III (beginning); cf. also sect. II, ch. I.

politics. Everywhere in Europe monarchies and principalities had been in temporary eclipse, but trust in kingship as the source of administration and law had persisted. Only in Italy had the influence of the highest authority, the emperor, shrunk while the papacy became absorbed by secular tasks in its own dominions. As a result of this and of the early development of municipal independence, the individual city-states of the fifteenth and sixteenth centuries regarded themselves as their own princes. They might continue as republics, or in a semiconstitutional way as a *signoria*. In a setting in which fragmentation of power was carried even further than in Europe's other turbulent and disrupted countries, usurpation of power became possible, and "tyrants"—rulers who governed in violation of still-existing traditional laws—emerged.

The rational empirical study of politics as well as the intensified observation of nature and of the world are important traits of the Renaissance. Yet for a long time these new concepts were not fully incorporated into the general thinking.

The institutional structure was not shaken. Even in Italy the basic institutions of Old Europe persisted through the Renaissance; new powers were accommodated alongside the old forces. The latter regained their old strength once the impetus of the Renaissance weakened in the later sixteenth century. This revival cannot be explained exclusively as Hispanization or as an effect of the Counter-Reformation, as has sometimes been done.

The humanists absorbed the philosophy, ethos, and institutional accomplishments of the ancients, especially of the Romans, more fully than had ever been done before. The leading scholar in the field of classical heritage, R. R. Bolgar, contrasts the attitude of former centuries that had regarded the Romans "as paragons of learning" with the attitude of the humanists who saw them "as paragons of human excellence."[43] Through numerous channels, though slowly, the impact of the new appraisal of the Romans made itself felt: in the military area, even, by way of the teaching of Neo-

[43] R. R. Bolgar, *The Classical Heritage and Its Beneficiaries* (Cambridge, 1954), p. 281.

Stoicism in both religious camps, in the disciplined attitude of statesmen such as Richelieu in the seventeenth century. Renaissance ideas penetrated the aristocratic–hierarchical world, without transforming it.

The Dynastic State

Municipalities and courts in Italy, including the papal court, vied in sponsoring Renaissance culture. In the north, because of the more limited development of municipal strength, the courts of the great dynasties and of their agnates played the leading part, though the role of the city patriciate should not be underestimated. Travels and migrations of artists and humanists and the dissemination of their attainments by means of the rapidly developing book trade added a new component to a common European civilization; cities like Nuremberg, Strasbourg, Basel, and Lyons were centers for the new interchange. In munificence and political weight they could not rival the dynastic states that dominated the configuration of European politics.

The interpretation of the age by historians has rightly centered on the great monarchies. Yet in no field has the concern with the modernity of the age played greater havoc with a true understanding of dynastic aims and of dynastic power. Only recently have stereotypes like "the new monarchy" or "the rise of the middle class" been discarded, thanks to the work of Jack Hexter, Helmut G. Koenigsberger, Russell Major, and J. H. Elliott.[44] Although the term *Renaissance monarchy* has been adopted, I prefer *the dynastic state,* since this term is less limited in time and since it indicates the main characteristic of the great monarchies.

Possessions and claims of the family had always been a basic element of royal and princely strength, but they had been embedded in a feudal system at the center of which was the king. Feudal attach-

[44] Cf. p. 39, n. 15, this volume; also A. J. Slavin, ed., *The "New Monarchies" and Representative Assemblies* (Boston, 1964), and a penetrating analysis in H. G. Koenigsberger's inaugural lecture at King's College, London, 1975, "Dominium Regale or Dominium Politicum et Regale."

ment was by no means dead—the Connétable of Bourbon justified his defection from Francis I in feudal terms—but the accumulated strength of the great ruling families had outstripped what was owed them by feudal allegiance. Matrimonial policy and succession treaties added to their power; their close ties with commercial and financial capitalism consolidated their position in a period when the output of the overseas mines, for Spain or via Spain, was a prerequisite for solvency of the crown.

Courts and capitals grew in strength, and in turn they contributed to royal power. New centers, such as Madrid, came into existence, and even an old city like Paris gained in reputation when the kings of France, who had lived for some time primarily in the Loire castles, settled there. The perambulatory way of living had not come to an end, but the capitals surpassed other places of residence. We should not regard this development as centralization in the modern sense, since newly acquired principalities retained their own identities. They expected the rulers to make regular appearances within their confines and to give their regions an equal chance. If the kings failed in this respect, as did the Hapsburgs in Catalonia, grave complications resulted. Neither can the consolidation of the dynastic state be equated with the emergence of the national state. In France the progress of the vernacular as a literary language was to some degree matched by the adoption of French as the official language, but the regional languages persisted. A contemporary commentator on this specific ordinance of 1539 remarked that regional languages could not be eliminated because "a Gascon does not know French."[45] The road toward full identification of crown and nation was a protracted one; in countries like England or Sweden the cooperation of crown and parliament in the rupture with Rome was to create a solid common basis.

With the exception of Elizabethan England, the foreign policy of the dynastic state very rarely pursued aims that can be called national. The dynastic state was a conglomerate of territories that the crown aimed to increase, mostly on the basis of legal claims, in order to outstrip its rivals. How else can the main conflict of the

---

[45] *Revue historique de droit Français et étranger* (1950), p. 574.

period, the Italian wars between the crowns of Spain and France, be explained? Eventually the contest between the crown of France and the Hapsburgs was to become the issue around which an emerging European system of states evolved, but this was still a long way off. Burckhardt's tempting phrase "the state as a work of art" has caused later historians to interpret the relations between the dynastic states as highly rational. Yet even among writers on politics, a concept like "the European balance of power" occurs rarely prior to the later seventeenth century. If a tendency in this direction existed among statesmen—and nobody can prove it—it certainly was pushed back by the religious conflicts.

Up to the middle of the seventeenth century, the dynastic state did not have at its disposal a thoroughly organized system of diplomacy, similar to the one that had existed among the states of the Italian Renaissance. Any reader of Garrett Mattingly's penetrating study will arrive at the conclusion that the establishment of permanent embassies throughout Europe was a slow process.[46] For a long time no continuity in diplomatic personnel existed. When Richelieu in 1616 was in charge of foreign affairs for the first time, he had to ask the envoys to send him copies of their instructions; none had been kept by the administration.

Finally, the instruments of warfare—the mercenary armies— were not exclusively in the hands of the crown, with the notable exception of the costly artillery. Nor were the troops permanently organized. The Roman concepts of fortitude and discipline were weighty contributions of humanism to warfare.[47] Yet their momentum was only to be felt in the course of the seventeenth century. They had their effect in the change to professional armed forces, "the military revolution," so ably described by Michael Roberts.[48] Eventually, by the late seventeenth century, the military entrepreneur was to be replaced by a standing army in the service of the prince. The search for "origins" must not lead us, as has happened, to regard the establishment of permanent military units by

[46] Garrett Mattingly, *Renaissance Diplomacy* (Boston, 1955/Baltimore, 1964).

[47] Gerhard Oestreich, "Der Roemische Stoizismus und die Oranische Heeresreform," in *Geist und Gestalt des fruehmodernen Staates* (Berlin, 1969).

[48] Michael Roberts, *The Military Revolution, 1560–1660* (Belfast, 1956).

the crown of France in the middle of the fifteenth century as the beginning of a standing army. These *companies de la grande ordinance* were primarily meant to incorporate the military vigor of the nobility into the service of the crown. Nobles served not only as officers, but also in the ranks.[49] Yet the aim to restrict the warfare of the seigneurs and the upkeep of their fortresses was not attained. How lightly these small formations weighed in the balance of warfare is evident in the two centuries of external and internal wars that followed.

"In well-organized and well-regulated states no individual, whoever he may be, can be permitted to have control over a large number of armed forces," argued Richelieu in 1627,[50] thus claiming the monopoly of force for the crown. The old feudal obligation toward a great lord had been largely replaced by "livery and maintenance," keeping a host of smaller nobles attached to a princely or baronial court. The personal connection had been transformed in this manner, but the sentiment of patronage and dependence remained as strong as ever. Our term for such a relationship is *client*. Contemporaries called themselves *servants*, or frequently even *créatures* ("creatures"). This term, borrowed from the ecclesiastical vocabulary, was much in vogue both in Italy and in France well into the seventeenth century and denotes the emphatic personal character of the tie.[51]

The internal administration was not bureaucratic in the modern sense. At the center, a topical arrangement was gradually introduced. In England reforms under Henry VIII strengthened the separation of "national" departments from the royal household, a separation that had begun in so-called medieval times. This further advance was decisive for initiating a topical arrangement.[52] Parallel developments can be traced on the Continent. In German territories a collegiate system was introduced, and in Hapsburg Spain councils

[49] Ph. Contamine, *Guerre, état et société à la fin du moyen age* (Paris, 1972).

[50] Vicomte Georges D'Avenel, *Richelieu et la monarchie absolue,* vol. II (Paris, 1884), p. 393.

[51] Cf. D. Gerhard, "Richelieu," in *Gesammelte Aufsaetze* (Gottingen, 1977), p. 127.

[52] G. R. Elton, *The Tudor Revolution in Government* (London, 1953).

either for some areas or for special affairs were gradually established, yet the distribution of functions was neither precise nor rational by modern standards. Such a statement is valid also for the
royal secretaries, later known as secretaries of state, who emerged in
France and soon also in other countries; they dealt with external as
well as with internal affairs. In addition, the old royal council of
feudal origin, composed of members of the high nobility, was still in
existence and at times exerted its influence. Joseph Strayer, who has
devoted most of his writings to the growth of the concept of supreme
power as a result of the revival of Roman law and the development
of a bureaucracy, nonetheless admits that after 1300, ''it took four to
five centuries for the European states to overcome their weaknesses.''[53] These ''weaknesses'' had been part of the social-
political structure of Old Europe.

The crown depended mainly on local officeholders. In Branden-
burg–Prussia, for instance, the central government penetrated the
cities with its own officials only in the late seventeenth century,
when the Great Elector established the office of the *Steuerrat*.[54] At the
same time, the office of lieutenant-general of police was created for
most major cities in France; prior to this period local self-help had
been largely in the hands of a *garde bourgeoise*. For the early seventeenth century the appraisal of Pàges, one of the most
knowledgeable on the internal history of France, is that ''the king
limits himself to administering justice, levying taxes and restoring
order where it is endangered . . . There is no royal administration,
only local administration exists.''[55]

Within the dynastic state regionalism and corporatism restrained
the actions of princely government. Because of these restrictions the
rise of so-called absolutism (i.e., effective and continuous control by

[53] Joseph R. Strayer, *On the Medieval Origins of the Modern State* (Princeton, 1970),
p. 57.

[54] Cf. pp. 127 ff., this volume, on the commissioners; the *Steuerrat* was a commissioner for the cities.

[55] G. Pagès, *Les institutions monarchiques sous Louis XIII et Louis XIV* (Paris, 1962),
p. 69. For functions and development of French offices, an excellent guide is provided by M. Marion, *Dictionnaire des institutions de la France aux 17e et 18e siècles* (Paris,
1928; reprint 1968).

the king's government) was delayed until the late seventeenth century. Prior to that period the countervailing forces made themselves constantly felt. The officials of the crown in the country who usually combined judicial and administrative functions were hemmed in not only by the rights of municipalities, feudal lords, and regional estates. Regional privileges often prevented outsiders from holding office; in many areas regional estates retained a hold on appointments. In numerous ways—for instance, by buying or inheriting office—officeholders tended to become a corporate group with a vested interest.[56] To be sure, they were mostly legally trained agents of the crown, which sometimes installed them by overriding regional claims, but they did not resemble a modern salaried bureaucracy. In not a few cases we might rather speak of a feudalization of offices.

No matter from which group the officeholders were originally recruited—whether from the gentry, as in England where the justices of the peace in the counties were mostly trained in London at the Inns of Court, or from the city patriciate, as often in Germany—by the sixteenth century they were established as a rather compact group. Access to this group was coveted by members of many layers of society. Montaigne even observed that the *noblesse de robe,* the holders of high office in the *parlements* in *robe longue* and in the financial courts of the same rank regarded themselves as a kind of Fourth Estate.[57]

In another administrative area it took Richelieu 10 years, because of the acquired rights to office, to change the navy into a centrally directed governmental agency. He eventually resigned himself not to accomplish fundamental reforms and accepted venality and heredity of offices. In his so-called *Political Testament* it was stated that "in an old monarchy the imperfections have become habitual, and the disorders have become, not without advantage, part of the order of the state."[58] Even in England where heredity of office was not legally established, the proprietary right to an office

[56] Gerhard, "Amtstraeger zwischen Krongewalt und Staenden," in *Gesammelte Aufsaetze.*

[57] Montaigne, *Essais,* ed. M. Rat (Paris, 1962), bk. I, ch. 23, p. 124.

[58] Last edition, ed. L. André (Paris, 1947), pt. I, ch. IV, sect. I, p. 234.

as to a "freehold" was generally accepted. For the first half of the seventeenth century, the English situation has been described in the following way:

> The means of appointment (usually by patrimony, patronage, purchase, or some combination of these), the creation of reversionary interests, the forms of tenure (particularly for life), pluralism and the performance of duties in absence (by official deputies or by underclerks and servants) . . . characterized every branch of central government, and every level within it except the highest.[59]

In one of the Hapsburg territories, in Styria, the lack of organs of the crown made it possible for the landholding nobility to sabotage the execution of a princely decree for almost a century.[60]

The dynastic state may be likened to a composite, often expanding colossus that could only act with difficulty. For fulfilling its tasks it depended not only on trained subordinates, but even more on the support of financiers and the cooperation of regional authorities, a cooperation that often was not forthcoming. Except in England, Castile, and Sweden the crown was not successful in rallying regional representatives for recurrent support in common assemblies. When common assemblies took shape—for instance, in the German territorial states—the individual representatives remained spokesmen of their special regions and corporate groups.[61]

Under the stress of warfare and increased taxation, the dynastic states in the middle of the seventeenth century eventually underwent what historians recently have defined as a crisis.[62] At that time

[59] G. E. Aylmer, *The King's Servants. The Civil Service of Charles I.* (London/New York, 1961), ch. III, sect. 8, "Entry and Service."

[60] Anton Kern, *Ein Kampf ums Recht. Grundherren und Weinbauern in der Steiermark im 16. und 17. Jahrhundert* (Graz, 1941).

[61] Gerhard, "Staendische Vertretungen und Land," in *Gesammelte Aufsaetze.*

[62] Trevor Aston, ed., *Crisis in Europe, 1560–1660* (London, 1965). A very substantial analysis of social–political conditions in Europe in this period and a rather skeptical appraisal of the "crisis" concept are in Henry Kamen, *The Iron Century. Social Change in Europe, 1550–1650* (New York, 1971). Th. K. Rabb, in *The Struggle for Stability in Early Modern Europe* (New York, 1975) has once more dealt with this "crisis in Europe" in a penetrating analysis and from a wider perspective. He relates these revolutions to an underlying loss of a common goal and of common convictions, and he traces this loss especially in art and literature after the end of the

several distinct uprisings took place in various European countries; in addition to the better known English Revolution and the Fronde in France, there were four regional revolts against the Hapsburg crown, in Portugal, Catalonia, Naples, and Sicily. In the Netherlands, only the death of William II forestalled an armed encounter between the House of Orange and the states of Holland. Undoubtedly these conflicts were caused by the greatly increased taxes imposed by the central government. They also revealed a fundamental difference in outlook between court and country, in the words of Trevor-Roper. The historians of the 1950s who discussed Trevor-Roper's thesis concluded that the cause of the conflict was not so much the growing court expenses but rather requests due to the rapid increase of the armed forces.

In the line of thought of this book, these events are the climax in a sequence of frequent conflicts within the dynastic state. The conflicts of the mid-seventeenth century were closely related to the acquisition of the monopoly of power by kings and princes. They differed in scope, but fundamentally not in motivation, from previous encounters of the kind.

Yet before the monarchies entered the critical test of the mid-seventeenth century, they had to face a much deeper crisis that shook their very foundation, a crisis of religion. It is time to ask what the period of the Reformation meant for Old Europe.

The Reformation and the Religious Wars

In the midst of his *German History in the Age of the Reformation,* Ranke pauses to remind his readers of the universal aspect of his story.[63] Through long periods, he remarks, "European civilization had been occupied with realizing in government and church, in

---

Renaissance. To him "all standards and institutions were open to questions and total overhaul," and this disillusionment paved the way for the acceptance of the new order of the centralized state by the end of the seventeenth century. It should be realized, however, that a potential conflict between locality and region on the one hand and the crown on the other hand was implicit in the very structure of Old Europe.

[63] Introduction to bk. VII.

literature and art the principles it had embraced. Suddenly we find ourselves in the midst of a universal commotion. A new position had to be taken. And yet everything depended on retaining the basis of civilization, on transmitting to subsequent centuries the results which previous generations had achieved." Thus Ranke describes the task that this book, too, tackles. It is concerned with continuity within Old Europe. As indicated at the outset, institutions are the very backbone of a civilization, and institutions and ideas are complementary. Was not the central institution of Western Christendom, the Roman Catholic church, shattered by the Reformation? And did not the new certitude at which the monk–professor in his lonely struggle had arrived, and his concept of the priesthood of all believers, attack, and for many Christians destroy, the basis of the church, the order of priesthood which was at the very center of the corporate structure of Europe?

We are dealing here with the Reformation as a period within the context of Old Europe, with the aims of the Reformers and with the immediate impact of the Reformation. Its potential consequences, whatever they were, in the later "modern" and ever more secularized Europe, are not relevant here. These potential consequences are not discernible in the over 100 years of religious conflicts that emanated from the Reformation. As to the Reformers themselves, we should try, in Ranke's words, to understand the new position which was taken, to inquire whether it differed fundamentally from the old principles of European civilization or whether it only transformed some of its institutions without abandoning these principles.

A. G. Dickens, to whom we owe a penetrating analysis of Reformers in both camps—an analysis of rare empathy—has rightly warned against dividing the Reformation into distinct currents. Instead, he has called it "an ocean in turmoil."[64] Let us ask the simple question, What was this turmoil about? To this question there is an equally simple answer: It was about religion, or, more specifically, about the meaning of the Christian religion. Granted that social conflicts, dynastic rivalries, and power politics became

[64] A. G. Dickens, *Reformation and Society in Sixteenth Century Europe* (London, 1966), p. 110.

enmeshed in the religious struggle, the fact remains that for more than a century the fighting in Europe was about religion and about the nature of the institutional church. This statement is valid for France and Germany as well as for Sweden and Poland; it can even be made for England.

From the very beginning, the Reformation—in this respect quite different from the Renaissance—affected all of Europe. Though connected in Germany with deeply felt grievances about exploitation from Rome, it immediately reached out into Switzerland and into the Netherlands and France, and soon into other European countries. Not since the time of the Reform Papacy have we met with a similar universal movement. Yet this time it was not carried forward by a well-anchored central institution; rather it resulted from the deep religious anxiety of one man, Martin Luther. What further proof do we need to show that religion was still at the very center of man's feelings?

Such an interpretation need not leave out of consideration various conditions that played into the hands of the Reformers, such as a national opposition to Rome, and the increasing desire of governments to gain control of the churches. Any religious movement was bound to draw strength from the ever-increasing participation of the laity in religious questions and from the opportunities opened up by the printing press. Hence Helmut Koenigsberger argues that, "despite the Reformers' hopes, none of the Reformation movements could ever be in a position to capture the central bastion of the old church, as the Cluny movement had done in the eleventh century, nor to take the place of the Catholic Church as the sole universal church of Western Christendom."[65] For us, it is more important that the Reformers and their followers consciously and unconsciously aspired to that goal. How could it have been otherwise, since Luther's religious experience—as well as, in a less challenging way, Zwingli's, and, in the next generation, Calvin's—originated in the very center of faith and led to a reinterpretation of fundamentals? It was this fact that made the pronouncements that had grown out of Luther's personally attained certitude spread like wildfire.

[65] "The Unity of the Church and the Reformation," in *Journal of Interdisciplinary History* (Spring 1971), p. 416.

What was at stake can best be shown by the testimony given by the two cardinal figues at the Diet of Worms in April, 1521. Here is the statement of Charles V when Luther had refused to recant and when the emperor announced that he would proceed against Luther as a notorious heretic:

> My predecessors as Emperors, archdukes of Austria, dukes of Burgundy, have been loyal sons of the Catholic church unto their death. For the honor of God and for the salvation of their souls they have defended and spread the faith. They have rendered to me the holy Catholic religion so that I live and die in it. . . . A simple monk, guided by his personal judgment, has taken a stand against the faith which all Christians have preserved through more than a thousand years, and he boldy contends that all Christians have erred until today.

And here are Luther's famous words:

> Unless I shall be convinced by Scripture and plain reason . . . my conscience is captive to the Word of God [*mein Gewissen im Worte Gottes gefangen*]. I cannot and will not recant, for to act against conscience is burdensome [*beschwerlich*], unwholesome [*unheilsam*], and dangerous [*und gefaehrlich*].

The absolute certainty at which Luther had arrived after years of lonely abandonment in the face of the *deus absconditus*, his confidence in salvation by faith only, was rooted in conscience. Yet *conscience* should not be interpreted in an emancipated, individualistic, modern way. Roland Bainton, in discussing the rejection of heretics by the Reformers, once remarked: "Conscience, the Reformers claimed, means nothing apart from *scientia; Gewissen* must be based on *Wissen*."[66] The evolution of the term *conscience* deserves further scrutiny. The French *conscience* still implies conscience as well as consciousness. In English and German the emancipation of *Gewissen* from *Wissen*, of conscience from consciousness, seems to have been a lengthy process. In Luther's language, *Gewissen* had not cut loose from *Wissen*. Luther's religion was the religion of the grace of God that is given to man, not as a result of human merit or of fulfilling

---

[66] Roland H. Bainton, *The Travail of Religious Liberty* (New York, 1951), introduction, p. 21.

the precepts of the church. It is, in the words of Karl Holl, "das ihm durch eine hoehere Ordnung Auferlegte, das Gemusste."[67] As such it is anchored in conscience, but conscience exists only in relation to God—in Luther's words, as "gut gewissen zu Gott."[68] Was Luther's conscience, then, as Charles V surmised, a personal judgment? As Luther stated, it was captive to the Word of God. For him *Wissen* and *Gewissen,* consciousness and conscience, were inextricably intertwined. All consciousness and conscience derived from the Word. The Word was not just Scripture, as Luther's position was later misinterpreted. The Word, he insisted against the Spiritualists, was not identical with the Holy Spirit. It manifested itself also in the means through which the Word worked: the Scripture, ordinances of God, such as baptism, and the preached Word of God. Luther came to reject the authority of pope and councils, and the emperor turned against him in horror. Yet Luther rejected them for the sake of a true understanding of the Christian message. Only very gradually—differing in this respect from Zwingli and Calvin—did Luther turn to reforming the church. By necessity, the Reformation movement led to reformed institutional churches, at bottom as universal in their goal as the old church.

Nobody will deny the tremendous upheaval that the Reformation effected. For centuries the Catholic church had been at the center of the social–political fabric. Luther's attack on the sacerdotal church eventually led to the abolition of the priesthood among Protestants; the indelible character of the priesthood disappeared. The endowments supporting countless private masses were eliminated. Luther's concept of the universal priesthood of all believers struck at the root of the monastic orders and led to their abolition. Saints and the veneration of saints were to vanish.

We ask: Which institutions in the countries of the Reformation replaced the one universal church? Leaving for the moment the

[67] Karl Holl, "Was verstand Luther unter Religion?" in *Gesammelte Aufsaetze zur Kirchengeschichte,* vol. I, *Luther* (Tübingen, 1932), p. 35.

[68] Quoted by Karl Holl in "Der Neubau der Sittlichkeit," in *"Gesammelte Aufsaetze zur Kirchengeschichte,* vol. I, p. 225, n. 2.

currents of a "Radical Reformation" aside, the answer has to be this: numerous territorial churches.

The very principle of the Reformation as interpreted by the Reformers required institutional bonds and institutional guidance. In the words of Ernst Troeltsch, "the Word, its fundament in the Bible, its manifestation in the sacraments [i.e., in baptism and communion] and its annunciation by preaching is a treasure [*Stiftungsschatz*] which exists independent of individuals and is of the institution's own."[69] Hence the Reformers, quite a few of whom were former priests and theologians and often humanistically or legally trained, were closely associated with theology and with the work of biblical humanism, despite the divergence between Luther and Erasmus in fundamentals of religion. As much as lax clerics had been derided and disdained, priests and monks had remained an essential part of the social–political structure and were held in high esteem. Protestant ministers, whose office required thorough theological training, were paid similar respect. Here and in the relation to government lies the marked difference between the Reformation and the innumerable groups—Anabaptists and Spiritualists—that stressed the prophetic calling and persisted as an undercurrent despite persecution from both Protestant and Catholic camps. In a masterful book George H. Williams has investigated the widespread network of the "Radical Reformation" in the sixteenth century,[70] and he contrasts it sharply with the "Magisterial Reformation" (i.e., the Reformation carried through in unison with the secular power, whether kings or princes or city magistrates—to use Luther's formulation, the *Christliche Obrigkeit*). The radicals, the so-called sects, were to have a great future. Many of the ideas and institutions that took shape after the later seventeenth century had already appeared among them. Nevertheless it is legitimate to refer to them as an undercurrent. Even in England the Puritans did not come to the forefront prior to the mid-seventeenth century. They had to be satisfied with membership in the Church of England, though later they broke away from the establishment at their own

[69] *Die Soziallehren der Christlichen Kirchen und Gruppen* (Tübingen, 1911/1923), ch. III, "Der Protestantismus," sect. I. "Das soziologische Problem," p. 449.

[70] George H. Williams, *The Radical Reformation* (Philadelphia, 1962).

volition. A state church was constituted as a result of the Protestant Reformation and a state church in different forms remained the rule in both Protestant and Catholic countries through the whole epoch of Old Europe, and beyond it. Even in most stages of the French Revolution a state church, different in forms and goals, persisted; religion had remained the core of a common civilization.

The state church entailed a close interpenetration of the church and the body politic. The religious schism, which endured contrary to the ecumenical expectations on both sides, strengthened the power of government in both Catholic and Protestant countries. Yet the relationship was a two-way affair. The fierceness of the religious wars in France and in central Europe was largely due to clerical influences on rulers and magistrates, in the Catholic and the Protestant camps alike, especially the Calvinist one.

The impact of the Reformation on social–political concepts has been investigated in great detail, particularly in relation to church structure. The congregational implications of the Calvinist churches have been rightly emphasized, as has the concept of predestination, which was of central significance to Calvin. Their effect may have been overstressed, due to the later urge for emancipation that was to become a fundamental characteristic of Modern Europe from the late seventeenth century on. Max Weber's thesis of the importance of Calvinism for the growth of capitalism is well known; it has been hotly debated and increasingly questioned. In a wider sense, including the realm of politics, the basic assumption was perhaps best formulated by Herbert Luethy when he claimed that Calvinism created "the type of free and responsible human being, the citizen in a new sense," that Calvinism "emancipated man from intellectual–spiritual subordination and fear."[71] Yet the potential individualistic distortion of Luther's "conscience" and of Calvin's "predestination" was for a long time balanced by the control exerted by the established churches.

Were secular life and secular occupation looked upon in a new and brighter light because of the Reformation? A few words about the much discussed problem of "calling" within the secular context

[71] "Die Ethik des Protestantismus," in *In Gegenwart der Geschichte* (Cologne, 1967), pp. 88 f.

seem to be pertinent to this question. Undoubtedly, the elimination
in Protestant countries of monastic life and of the sacerdotal
character of priesthood added to the dignity of secular occupation.
Protestant church historians have contrasted Luther's concept of
calling, as related to secular work, with the notions of order and
estate in the social–political theory of previous centuries. Karl Holl
has even concluded that Thomas Aquinas knew of a service within
the realm of natural order, but not of a calling.[72] Furthermore,
within the movement of the Reformation the differences between
Lutheranism and Calvinism have been duly emphasized by
historians. Luther accepted worldly government and the corporate
order in their own right, though he regarded government as being
under the obligation to protect the Word. To fight the corruption of
the Christian message by its identification with revolutionary social
programs, he took his stand with the princes against the peasants.
This stand contributed to the conservatism of German Lutheranism. Calvinism, on the contrary, often had to fight for its existence in conflict with royal authority; its connection with
municipal liberty was closer than that of the Lutheran Reformation.

Whatever the cause of the potential militant stand of Western
European Protestantism, it implied no encouragement of either
emancipated economic individualism or purely secular politics.
Such tendencies antedated the Reformation without having pro-
foundly changed the corporate order or the links between religion,
law, and politics. If anything, these ties became even stronger in the
period of the Reformation and the religious wars. Certainly the
"Elizabethan world picture"[73] had no room for emancipated
humanity; as far as we meet with individuals apparently completely
absorbed by the striving for worldly success, I accept Jack Hexter's
observation that they did so in part because "they felt at their back
the burning heat of religious conflagration."[74]

In the century following the Reformation no basic change in at-

---

[72] "Die Geschichte des Wortes Beruf" in *Gesammelte Aufsaetze zur Kirchengeschichte,* vol. II (Tübingen, 1932), p. 203.

[73] E. M. W. Tillyard, *The Elizabethan World Picture* (London, 1944).

[74] J. H. Hexter, "Factors in Modern History," in *Reappraisals in History* (London, 1961), p. 43.

titude toward the social–political order can be found. Those who tend to interpret the Reformation as leading up, for good or for evil, to a later emancipated humanity, might well ponder Karl Holl's warning with regard to Luther's religion as a religion born of conscience: "This is an autonomy of its own, not to be regarded as an imperfect stage toward the autonomy of the Enlightenment."[75] It was an autonomy grounded in religion and it was contained by the established churches, whose most forward-moving founder, Calvin, had declared that God's children are gathered in the bosom of the church to be nourished by her help and to be guided by her motherly care.[76] The churches kept their position in political life and their leadership in institutions of learning. It is characteristic that not just where the episcopal office was retained, as in England and Sweden, but also in most other Protestant countries, at least a rudimentary representation of prelates and ecclesiastical foundations continued in the assemblies of estates. Often university representation was adjoined to it, and, as previously remarked, divinity held its high rank among the faculties well into the eighteenth century.

One of the best evaluations of the place of the Reformation within the course of European history was made by Hermann Heimpel when he resumed Ernst Troeltsch's probing. I fully accept his statement that "the Christian Civilization in its supernaturalistic character was not destroyed by the Reformation, but rather maintained. Luther and Early Protestantism maintained the medieval concept of the church. The answers of the Reformers are answers to old questions." I am not so certain, on the other hand, that Heimpel is right when he remarks that the spiritualization of religion that the Lutheran Reformation entailed made it more vulnerable to secularism.[77] In fact, the express secularism of the Enlightenment took its victorious course in Catholic and Protestant countries alike. But before this new epoch dawned, governments

[75] "Was verstand Luther unter Religion?" in *Luther*, p. 110.

[76] Calvin, *Institution* (French ed. 1560), bk. IV, ch. 1, "De la vraye église."

[77] Hermann Heimpel, "Ueber die Epochen der mittelalterlichen Geschichte" and "Luthers weltgeschichtliche Bedeutung," in *Der Mensch in seiner Gegenwart* (Gottingen, 1954/1957), pp. 56, 157 f.

and churches, though split and fighting each other in one of the most ferocious and most protracted series of wars in European history, once more tightened the old social–political structure under the banner of the churches.

For about 100 years, from the middle of the sixteenth century to the middle of the seventeenth, the religious element was either paramount or at least a strong component in the internal conflicts of European countries. Likewise it was a main element in the rivalries between states. The two aspects cannot be kept apart. The universal claims of revived Catholicism and of Calvinism especially knew of no bounds; because of the solidarity within each confession, struggles about religious uniformity inside a country invited interference from the outside. The emerging dynastic states were too weak—most of all, they still lacked the monopoly of force—to hinder the backing of their organized minority churches by other powers. This is particularly true for the later sixteenth century, the period of the so-called Counter-Reformation. The strength of confessional conflicts and of their international ties is apparent until the middle of the seventeenth century. The religious struggle was the paramount element in the conflagration in central Europe known as the Thirty Years' War. Only as a result of the conflict between the confessions did the dynastic states acquire full control over their territories; only at the end of this period, in the late seventeenth century, did the often antedated "system of European states" make its appearance.

The term *Counter-Reformation*, as just used, is hardly adequate to describe the depth of the Catholic reform or the strength of its organization. The term is a late creation of historical scholarship. In the later 1870s Ranke, perhaps in view of Catholic strength in the *Kulturkampf*, replaced the previously used plural, which had denoted specific counteractions in individual territories, by a singular, "the age of Counter-Reformation."[78] A movement from within, which had partly preceded the Reformation, was to last until the seven-

[78] Paul Joachimsen, in vol. VI of his historical–critical edition (Munich, 1926).

teenth century, when it reached its climax in France. It reformed the priesthood; at the same time it aimed at influencing society. It educated its higher ranks and through them attempted to mitigate by works of charity the unspeakable hardships and poverty of the common people. Under the direction of the papacy, the Council of Trent had clarified the dogmatic base and tightened the institutional arrangements of the church. Like Calvinism on the Protestant side, Catholicism was strengthened by disciplined leadership, particularly of the Jesuits.

Most of all, because of the character of the institutional territorial church, governments on both sides backed the efforts of priesthood and ministry, and it may well be, as A. G. Dickens has stated, that "the general fear of social and religious chaos helped Catholicism far more than it helped Luther and Calvin."[79] The Catholic governments, though, whether we think of Spain or France, interpreted the ecclesiastical regulations in their own way; even less than in previous centuries were they willing to be mere handmaidens of the papacy.

Intolerance was a constituent factor of the institutional church, which remained the core of civilization as interpreted by different governments. The ferocity of the confessional conflicts surpassed those of former times. It is hardly necessary to call to mind the role of the Inquisition or the persecution of witches, which reached its height in these centuries, and in both camps.[80]

The ruler—mostly king or prince—was to decide about the religion of a country or a territory; at times a major goal in the protracted struggle was to win over the highest authority. From the fight against a "tyrant"—a ruler who by his stand on religion had broken his pledge to guard the law of the land—a very influential literature on the right of resistance emerged. This literature added strength to the position of estates and municipalities. In France's

---

[79] A. G. Dickens, *The Counter-Reformation* (London, 1969), p. 33.

[80] H. R. Trevor-Roper, *The European Witch-Craze of the Sixteenth and Seventeenth centuries* (New York 1965/1969), relates the persecution to special "incompatibilities" of traditions and regions, which, according to him, characterized this age in contrast to former periods. Th. K. Rabb (cf. n. 62) explains the witch-craze as an indication of the "disillusionment" of the age.

murderous religious wars even the bonds of corporate society were temporarily broken by the countrywide formation of religious associations, regardless of estate or region[81]—a foreshadowing of the later voluntary association that was to become a mainstay of the modern age.

Looking at the period of religious wars from the secular side, it appears to be of an ambiguous nature. On the one hand, the factionalism of magnates, nobles, and municipalities persisted in unabated strength. Contemporary Italian writers, aware of the tradition of the violent internal struggles of their city-states, regarded the conflict in France as a mere struggle for power between high-ranking individuals.[82] On the other hand, for the heads of the great dynastic states the fight for religion was inextricably intertwined with full control over their territories—or, rather, over what in this period came to be known as their "state"—and with their European position and reputation.

In the Catholic as well as the Protestant camp, princes as heads of the state church increased their control over ecclesiastical matters. Not only did this add to their strength, it also led to exalting the role and position of the kings. A theory of the divine right of kings was formulated by the seventeenth century.[83] It attempted to further the consolidation of the baroque kingdoms and principalities that mark the mid-seventeenth century.

Courts and court life mirrored this process. Henry IV of France promoted the training of the nobility in fencing and dancing. Richelieu's relentless fight against dueling, though not fully successful, aimed at prohibiting what often amounted to large-scale attacks on nobles by other nobles. At the same time Italian influence and the impact of the Catholic reform led to the first salons. The way for the domestication of the nobility was thus prepared. Special

[81] H. G. Koenigsberger, "The Organization of Revolutionary Parties in France and the Netherlands during the Sixteenth Century," in *Estates and Revolutions* (Ithaca, N.Y., 1971).

[82] Cf. the criticism of Davila's "Storia delle guerre civili di Francia" in Ranke's *Franzoesische Geschichte,* vol. 5.

[83] Cf. William F. Church, *Richelieu and Reason of State* (Princeton, 1972), pt. I, sect. 3, for the emergence of the concept of divine right of kings as furthering the idea of reason of state.

academies for the training of the nobles with the aim of furthering gentility are indicative of this new development. Full integration of the aristocracy into the state was the goal; it was attained only after this period.

The sense for form and discipline that permeated the Catholic Reformation transcended its boundaries, although the Catholic courts of Spain and France were leading in the arts. Baroque art elevated princely government; the palaces of the rulers were as much a concern of great architects and sculptors as were the churches. Even more than previously in the Renaissance religion and secular elements intermingled. Yet the splendor of court and court life was not complemented by full control over the country before the later seventeenth century, when governments systematically applied themselves to this task.

The universal aspect of the religious–political struggle can hardly be overestimated. The Hapsburgs, especially their Spanish branch, regarded themselves a protectors of Christendom. Philip II was accused by his enemies of aiming at a universal monarchy. By this time the opposition to such a threat was based on the assumption of the coexistence of independent states within Christendom. It may have been no accident that among the powers threatened by Spain this position was adopted by England, Europe's most homogeneous country.[84]

In France, which almost disintegrated in the religious conflict, this very danger rallied ever stronger support around the king, especially of lawyers and political writers, in the interest of French unity. In this context Bodin formulated the term *sovereignty* without abandoning the idea of the king as guardian of the law. Both within and outside of France, the concept of sovereignty became the main instrument for establishing the place of ultimate decision in the body politic. In this way it prepared the rise of what historians usually call *absolute power*. Eventually Richelieu subjugated the op-

---

[84] In 1570 Sir Thomas Wilson published a translation of Demosthenes' orations against Philip of Macedonia as "most needful to be read in these dangerous days of all them that love their country's liberty." There is an interesting parallel 235 years later when Barthold Georg Niebuhr dedicated his translation to Czar Alexander of Russia as to the champion of the European states against Napoleon.

posing forces and established the exclusive military power of the crown. Yet both Richelieu and Bodin are far removed from a belief in the autonomy of the emerging state. They realized that rulers had to act pragmatically and, in the interest of the state, sometimes had to give in to "necessity." Neither Bodin nor Richelieu glorified "reason of state," as they surrounded it by precepts of law and ethics. They were following the Neo-Stoic concept of the disciplined character of the statesman and of his disciplinarian task.[85]

France's deadliest enemy was another Catholic power, the Hapsburgs in Spain and Austria, whose increasing pressure made itself felt for almost a century. Yet even in the midst of the struggle common ecumenical goals were not abandoned. The idea of a crusade against the Turk, a recurrent threat in the East, played a part when Charles VIII in 1494 started the Italian war in the hope that Naples would give him a foothold for a campaign to make his title King of Jerusalem, as inherited from Angevin times, a reality. Almost 150 years later—in the midst of that open war against Spain that was to decide the configuration of European power politics for a long time to come—Louis XIII cried out: "I wish the Turk were in Madrid, then Spain would be forced to conclude peace and we could join hands to wage war on the Sultan."[86]

At the same time, in the late 1630s, a treatise by the Duc de Rohan, *De l'intérêt des princes et états de la Chrétienté,* was published. It has rightly been regarded as one of the earliest systematic appraisals of the European states.[87] Yet its title should warn us that the purely pragmatic approach to power politics was far from dominant. The princes had not yet been replaced by the states, and *Europe*—a term that gained further ground in this period—had not yet taken the place of *Christendom.* Gustavus Adolphus of Sweden, always mindful of the extension of Swedish power, had his daughter instructed in her duties as his prospective successor by a Latin treatise of the thir-

---

[85] Church, *Richelieu,* and Gerhard, "Richelieu." Oestreich, "Der Roemische Stoizismus" has shown the influence of Justus Lipsius on the spread of Neo-Stoic concepts.

[86] D'Avenel, *Richelieu,* vol. V (1890), p. 812.

[87] Friedrich Meinecke, *Die Idee der Staatsraeson in der Neueren Geschichte* (Munich, 1924; English trans. [*Machiavellism*], New Haven, 1957), bk. I, ch. VI.

teenth century by Aegidius Romanus, one of the "Mirrors of Princes."[88] Is it not of similar significance that Richelieu, while relentlessly forging French unity under the crown, wanted his king to adopt the cognomen "the Just," in the succession of Louis IX the Saint?

---

[88] Wilhelm Berges, *Die Fuerstenspiegel des Hohen und Spaeten Mittelalters* (Leipzig, 1938), p. 327.

5

Incipient Emancipation amidst
the Persistence of the Old Order
MID-SEVENTEENTH TO
LATE EIGHTEENTH CENTURIES

None of the movements of the previous centuries had challenged the basis of the social–political order and its underlying concepts, despite the long-lasting disruption of the religious wars. Once more it must be emphasized that the Reformers' ecumenical aim had been to regain the original Christian animus; it was not their goal to establish the autonomy of the individual. By the end of the seventeenth century we meet with a very different attitude, with a tendency toward secularism; simultaneously economic and political conditions began to change. As a result the traditional social-political structure came increasingly under attack. It is the task of this chapter to analyze the change that led to the disruption of Old Europe. Many factors shared in the emergence of a new, "modern" Europe—the intellectual movement, the altered economic conditions, the political transformation that was accomplished by the so-called absolutist government, and the English Revolution, which in two decades of religious–political upheaval shattered the traditional

111

fabric of government. To ascribe first cause to any one of them would be presumptuous; they have to be seen as a whole, initiating a new epoch together.

The Scientific Revolution and the Shaping of the Enlightenment

Gustavus Adolphus had been unsuccessful in having his daughter study, along with Lutheran orthodoxy, one of the contemporary editions of Aegidius Romanus' "Mirror of Princes." After Christina had come of age and prior to her conversion to Catholicism she was instructed by René Descartes. It was Descartes who eventually replaced Aristotle, if only after a protracted struggle. Aristotle and his commentators were a part of Isaac Newton's education at Cambridge as late as the 1660s; in Paris Cartesianism could not be taught at the university prior to the death of Louis XIV. R. W. Southern, in his discussion of the great scholastic textbooks of the twelfth century, mentions their extraordinarily long survival in the curriculum of European universities. He remarks: "The end of their undisputed usefulness in the seventeenth century marks the end of the Middle Ages more decisively than the Renaissance or the Reformation"[1]—an assertion that, except for the term *Middle Ages,* I fully accept.

Cartesian philosophy was an integral part of that great process that stretches, if not from Copernicus, from Galileo to and beyond Newton, which we now call the Scientific Revolution. By establishing the autonomy of reason, Descartes initiated the first of

[1] *The Making of the Middle Ages* (Oxford, 1953/1961), p. 205. Even more pronounced about the effect of the Scientific Revolution is Herbert Butterfield in the introduction to his *The Origins of Modern Science* (London, 1957): "Since that revolution overturned the authority in science not only of the Middle Ages but of the ancient world—since it ended not only in the eclipse of scholastic philosophy but in the destruction of Aristotelian physics—it outshines everything since the rise of Christianity and reduces the Renaissance and Reformation to the rank of mere episodes, mere internal displacements, within the system of medieval Christendom." For the interrelation of physics and astronomy with moral philosophy, see pp. 114 ff., this volume.

the "emancipations" that eventually became the most outstanding characteristic of the next centuries. Neither Galileo nor Descartes was bent on challenging the church, and from Descartes to Newton and Leibniz the new science and the new philosophy aimed at remaining in harmony with religious truth. Yet whether in astronomy or in philosophy or in physics, they insisted that their realm was an independent one. They could proceed to a belief in God as the creator of truth, as did Descartes, which even made him suspect to the *philosophes* of the next century. Nevertheless Descartes' *cogito ergo sum* was a definite break with Anselm of Canterbury's *credo ut intelligam,* which had remained the premise of thinking in previous centuries. Eventually the tie between theology and the other disciplines would be cut, and they would come into their own.

The underlying fundamental change has best been expressed by Basil Willey: "Interest was now directed to the *how,* the manner of causation, not its *why,* its final cause. . . . It was a general transference of interest from metaphysics to physics, from the contemplation of Being to the observation of Becoming."[2] To be sure, this was a lengthy process. Yet very soon the impact of the emerging new sciences made itself felt, both in the character of institutions of learning and in a changed interpretation of Christian religion.

The academies came into their own during the later seventeenth century. Of these institutions, rather than of the universities, it can be said that the urge for knowledge was a main cause for their formation. Though welcomed and eventually institutionalized by governments, they grew out of free associations of gentlemen–scholars. Some of these scholars felt like Descartes, who, according to his own testimony, heartily disliked the occupation of writing books, yet write they did. From the beginning, they exchanged their findings from country to country. Constant communication resulted from both the method of their studies and the purpose of their scholarship. Theory and experiment entered into the indissoluble union characteristic of modern science. Leonardo

[2] Basil Willey, *The Seventeenth Century Background* (Cambridge, 1934/New York, 1953), ch. I, sect. I, pp. 14, 16.

had headed in the same direction, yet only now a community was forged that strove to share each new finding. Investigation on the basis of rational analysis and experiment came to be regarded as a common enterprise in the advance of knowledge. Moreover, scholars realized that scientific progress meant increased control over the forces of nature. The purpose of the official publication of the Royal Society, the *Philosophical Transactions,* was put forth in the Introduction of 1664: "communicating to such as apply their studies and endeavours that way, such things as discovered and put in practice by others."[3] In line with this statement and purpose the first numbers of the *Journal des Savants* of 1665 published translations of the papers from the *Philosophical Transactions.* These "ingenious" gentlemen were, as the first contemporary historian of the Royal Society noted, "men of freer lives" and hence not encumbered with "dull and unavoidable employment." Christopher Hill rightly concludes that they could approach technological problems in a more detached way than craftsmen, who only gradually and late became involved in the new technology.[4] We must not antedate the latter development, though English scholars convincingly have shown that a new type of flexible grammar school—the so-called "Dissenting Academies," which were open to Noncomformists—prepared the way for modern industry. Characteristically, most of the scientists kept aloof from the universities. The greatest, like Leibniz, felt that a professorship would limit the range of their activities and of their influence. The universities retained their inherited structure and the close relationship of the "arts" (i.e., the humanities) with theology.

It is impossible to fasten any of our modern labels of a special discipline on men like Copernicus or Galileo. The "Copernican revolution"—in progress only since the mid-seventeenth century, about a century after Copernicus' death—meant a break with the Christian–Aristotelian world picture, since no barriers had yet been erected between physics and cosmology, between science and moral philosophy. Early in the century John Donne had conjured up the

---

[3] Charles R. Weld, *A History of the Royal Society,* vol. I (New York, 1975), p. 180. Sprat's history of the Royal Society, published in 1667, is entitled *The History of the Royal Society of London for the Improving of Natural Knowledge.*

[4] *Reformation to Industrial Revolution* (New York, 1967), pt. III, sect. II, end.

mechanistic and atomistic implications of the new world picture in often-quoted verses:

> 'Tis all in pieces, all coherence gone;
> All just supply, and all relation;
> Prince, subject, father, son, are things forgot,
> For every man alone thinks he hath got
> To be a Phoenix, and that then can be
> None of that kind, of which he is, but he.[5]

The cosmological order of the spheres, as viewed by Aristotle and incorporated into theological–philosophical teaching, had envisaged a finite universe. Though the earth, in contrast to the perfect spheres, had been regarded as imperfect, creation had been seen as centering on humanity. Now the fundamental change "from the closed world to the infinite universe"[6] turned the stable terrestrial scene into just one more planet in a universe without limit. The essential distinction between perfect heavenly bodies and the imperfect earth was destroyed; the earth was placed, in the words of Galileo, "in heaven, whence your philosophers have exiled it."[7]

It cannot be our task to analyze the transformation of consciousness and conscience that became apparent by the end of the seventeenth century. Paul Hazard has done that in his masterful *La crise de la conscience européenne.*[8] However, some of the concomitant changes that contributed to the new, "modern" outlook should be mentioned. The Europeans began to become fully aware of the implications of the discoveries: that the earth contained a multitude of different people (the term *civilizations* made its appearance much later) who deserved being studied in their own right. Simultaneously historical perception underwent a fundamental change. The Christian framework of history, within which the Incarnation had been the central event, was abandoned. The pragmatic–empirical

[5] John Donne, in *Anniversaries:* First Anniversary (1611) lines 213–218.

[6] Alexandre Koyré, *From the Closed World to the Infinite Universe* (New York, 1957).

[7] Galileo, Mathematical Collections and Translations, trans. by Th. Salisbury (1661); quoted in Willey, *Seventeenth Century Background,* p. 27, n. 17.

[8] *La crise de la conscience européene* (Paris, 1935).

interpretation of the history of the individual states, which had already guided Machiavelli and Guicciardini, found its counterpart on a larger scene. Eventually, by the eighteenth century, the whole of human history was seen as a continuing process, no longer *sub specie aeternitatis.*

In the late seventeenth century, the advent of religious toleration followed a period of dogmatic rigidity and violent and destructive religious conflicts. Nowhere had they been more cataclysmic than in England in the revolution of midcentury, which almost tore the country asunder. Here the religious struggle had been combined with a political conflict. At times it had brought to the fore the Levelers, who were social–religious extremists; their vision of a new social order—"the world turned upside down," as Christopher Hill has described it[9]—foreboded later revolutions. By the end of the century, when the monarchy had been restored, in England as well as in other countries most erstwhile heretics of the Radical Reformation, among them the Puritan dissenters, were tolerated. They could establish their own institutions, though in a position politically and socially inferior to that of members of the state church.

Dilthey has called the change to tolerance one of the greatest turning points in European history, and with the confidence of the dawning twentieth century he has added, "Philosophy and science furnished the power by which the crisis was overcome and the European mind was able to advance."[10] Neohumanists and Neo-Stoicists had indeed long since prepared the rulers for a policy of greater tolerance, born of conviction. Nevertheless the final victory of tolerance was rather, in Lawrence Stone's words, "not a triumph of moral principle over political expediency, but of political expediency over religious principle."[11]

By the end of the century the religious attitude was confronted by the change "from the closed world to the infinite universe." In religion, as in many other orbits, currents and traditions that had formerly led a secondary existence now came to the fore. One of

[9] Christopher Hill, *The World Turned Upside Down* (New York, 1972).

[10] Wilhelm Dilthey, "Leibniz und sein Zeitalter" (written around 1902), in *Gesammelte Schriften,* vol. III (Leipzig, 1927), p. 9.

[11] Lawrence Stone, *The Causes of the English Revolution* (London, 1972), p. 83.

them was the concept of the Great Chain of Being. The Platonic interpretation of the universe as an entity in which every potentiality of being finds its realization had not been forgotten in former centuries. In particular, the hierarchical order in the Chain of Being[12] had been accepted—yet the Christian message of salvation and redemption had overshadowed the inherently pantheistic outlook of Neoplatonism. The concept of a limitless universe now became associated with an undogmatic affirmative religion as it had been adumbrated by humanists and Renaissance philosophers. The religious concern of scientists like Leibniz or Newton is apparent in their unflinching endeavors for a theodicy. In their thought, however, humanity lost its central place in creation; it became part of a universe in which under the laws of nature every being was part of an ever new realization of being.

The gulf that had separated the heavenly bodies and the imperfect earth had been bridged by the new cosmology. Yet traces of older views persisted; the heavenly firmament had not lost its awe-inspiring character. Witness Kant at the end of the eighteenth century, when he postulated that humanity was guided by the moral law within and the starred sky above. A residue of the old Aristotelian concept of the pure spheres can be discerned in the idea of a life of more perfect beings on other planets.[13] Thus deism became a substitute religion, even penetrating the established churches.

The metaphysical component of the new philosophy was more and more abandoned. The *philosophes,* its popularizers and propagandists, like the whole eighteenth-century movement of the Enlightenment, were firmly grounded on this earth. Some of its representatives were indeed closely wedded to a mechanistic interpretation of nature; there was no room for metaphysics. Theirs was a truly secular approach; emancipation from revealed religion constituted the basis of their thinking. Whether we see the Enlightenment, in Peter Gay's telling words, as an epoch of "recovery of nerve," or whether, on the contrary, with Carl Becker and others

---

[12] Arthur O. Lovejoy, *The Great Chain of Being* (Cambridge, Mass., 1936/1964).

[13] Immanuel Kant, *Allgemeine Naturgeschichte und Theorie des Himmels*, 4th ed. (Zeitz, 1808), Dritter Teil, "Enthaelt eine Vergleichung zwischen den Einwohnern der Gestirne."

we regard the Enlightenment's belief in one humankind and in progress as a secularized version of the Christian heritage[14] the fact remains that secularism is its key note. The philosophes did not regard this turn as a break, but as an emancipation.

Emancipated individuals believed in reason; their confidence in reason was nourished by a change in humanity's relation with nature. The age-old feeling of fear and uncertainty ceased when humans increasingly learned how to control nature.[15] Max Weber has coined the term *disenchantment* (*Entzauberung*) for the modern world, and he has claimed rationality as the trait distinguishing the West from other civilizations. This characterization is valid only for the modern period.

In the realm of thought the eighteenth century prepared the way for the application of the new science, for never-ending industrial and technological revolutions. The emancipated became emancipators, with a zeal and a success hitherto reserved to the realm of religion. The Enlightenment, aided by improved communication, spread rapidly by means of the book trade. Most of all, it counted on a widely enlarged reading public. Periodicals, dictionaries, and encyclopedias, ranging from Bayle's *Dictionnaire historique et critique* to the *Grande Encyclopédie,* are manifestations of the transformation from the corporate order to the new, modern way of life in European history, to the "society" and to the "public." Economic and political changes cleared the way. Once more we are faced by the interplay of conditions and attitudes; we must refrain from monocausal explanation. It is time to turn to the social, economic, and political changes of the period. They tell of the coming of a new age.

The Economy

Late-eighteenth-century England witnessed the breakthrough of the Industrial Revolution. It meant, in the words of W. W.

---

[14] Peter Gay, *The Enlightenment. An Interpretation,* vol. II (New York, 1969); Carl L. Becker, *The Heavenly City of the Eighteenth Century Philosophers* (New Haven, 1932).
[15] Keith V. Thomas, *Religion and the Decline of Magic* (London, 1971).

Rostow,[16] the "takeoff" that assured the self-sustaining growth of entrepreneurial capital. We have to ask what the preparatory stage for this process was, and whether it initiated a fundamental transformation of the economy.

Since the latter half of the seventeenth century, the circulation of money had grown considerably. Largely as a result of the increase in taxation, the common people needed more cash; in this way they were indirectly more tied to the market economy. In times of depression they were heavily overburdened. Around 1700 some of the most thoughtful observers, such as Marshal Vauban, even suggested a return to payment in kind, as it was customary in the case of the tithe.[17] Yet in the end governments were able to carry on, at least in the advanced countries of Western Europe.

Contemporaries were aware of the role played by commercial capitalism. They observed the advance in shipping and foreign trade as the oustanding trait of Holland and England, which around 1700 were referred to as the maritime powers in the diplomatic vocabulary. In England the government had had its share in this development. The Navigation Laws of the mid-seventeenth century had brought promotion of shipping and protection of English foreign trade to its climax, and trade within England was facilitated by the improvement of roads and canals and by a low rate of interest. Holland and England were leading also in the refinement of banking techniques that facilitated the discounting of bills of exchange and enlarged the market for shares on the newly developing stock exchange. Consolidation and parliamentary control of English governmental debt added to the confidence in the economy.

The changes of the late seventeenth century in trade and finance mirrored the transformation that England had undergone under the impact of the preceding revolutionary upheaval. Once political security had again been attained, the aristocracy became ever more strongly involved in the demands and possibilities of a market economy. Governmental policy centered increasingly on the promotion of British trade; the union with Scotland has to be seen on both sides within this context. A widening home market and a flourishing

[16] W. W. Rostow, *The Stages of Economic Growth* (Cambridge, 1960).

[17] Marshal Vauban, *Projet d'une dixme royale,* ed. E. Coornaert (Paris, 1933).

overseas trade created the basis for a prosperous economy. The "middle ranks"—independent craftsmen or individuals under contract to merchants—had already played a significant part in the great mid-seventeenth-century upheaval of the English Revolution, not as a conscious middle class, as the Neo-Marxian stereotype would have it, but rather in conjunction with other groups. By the eighteenth century the middle ranks became important as customers as well as producers. Long unified and rather small in size, England presented a consolidated national market in advance of the Continent. According to a mid-eighteenth-century English calculation undertaken prior to the Industrial Revolution, more people were engaged in trade and manufacture than in agriculture.[18]

The middle groups, largely composed of Nonconformists, lived at the periphery of an aristocratic world of patronage that they did not challenge. Most of all, their way of living and producing had not changed; under the putting-out system the family and the small shop remained the working units. Factories were few, and only a small amount of capital was invested in industrial equipment.

The growth of manufactures was paralleled by changes in agriculture. Extension of arable land, largely by way of enclosures; the disappearance of the common lands; improved agricultural technique, particularly in crop rotation; and cultivation of new feed crops that made winter feeding in the barn possible—these were some of the advances of the seventeenth and eighteenth centuries in England, producing a higher yield. In many cases the village commune was fatally weakened; tenant farmers and farm laborers took the place of independent yeomen. This process, sometimes referred to as the Agricultural Revolution, was a preparatory stage to the Industrial Revolution.

In eastern Europe the large feudal estates, managed with serf labor, continued to export grain and naval stores, but their operations were not businesslike. In most areas agriculture remained untouched by English agronomy; only in the mid-eighteenth century is some progress noticeable in central Europe, especially in Prussia.

Apart from Holland, France had the greatest share in overseas ventures among the Continental countries. Yet in France we find,

[18] Harold Perkin, *The Origins of Modern English Society 1780–1880* (London, 1969/1972), p. 31.

as in a paradigm, the strong traditional barriers against industrial capitalism that had been built into the social–political structure of Old Europe. When in the second third of the eighteenth century the economy began to take an upward turn, regional manufactures advanced strongly, but notwithstanding Colbert's efforts under Louis XIV, the country had not developed a unified home market. Moreover, the putting-out system, which relied largely on poorly paid rural labor, remained the rule, and to a large extent capital investments went, as in previous centuries, into land and offices. Besides, in most parts of France a proprietary regime, frequently of absentee owners, prevailed in the countryside and this encumbered the cultivator with heavy obligations. The village commune and the common lands persisted; they supported the poor while restricting the well-to-do peasant.

It may well be that the large percentage of Nonconformists in England's middle ranks contributed to the spread of capitalist thinking, as the Weber thesis postulates. Undoubtedly the conviction of the dignity of labor, often underpinned by the religious concept of "calling," and a rather uninhibited view of the realities of commercial capitalism, as already shown by Calvin, facilitated the economic development of the northwestern European countries. A growing stress on discipline, however, and the professionalization of services can be found in much of Europe. Besides, the "capitalist" English landowners of the eighteenth century were rarely Dissenters.

The whole development ought rather to be seen within the wider context of the change of ideas sketched in the first section of this chapter, which in many fields implied a transition to quantitative thinking.[19] In an age of science, that endeavored to deal with human relations in mathematical terms, quantitative methods also became the tool of government; statistics were put at its disposal. This enlarged the understanding of the economic process. Previously the economic policy eventually called *mercantilism* either had been limited to balancing competing interests, or had been concerned with supporting especially promising sectors of the economy. Foreign trade and some branches of manufacture had been particularly promoted, and the commercial competition had even led to

---

[19] Cf. also pp. 70 ff., this volume.

warfare for economic reasons, as between the English and the Dutch and between the French and the Dutch in the later seventeenth century. Yet it was not until 1700 that the economy of France was envisaged as an interrelated whole,[20] and not until the mid-eighteenth century that the Physiocrats conceived economic circulation as a unified system.

How profound the underlying change in ideas about human relations was, can best be seen in the altered concept of property.[21] Formerly it had been connected with function and authority, with the control over a house; wealth had been seen foremost in landed estates endowed with authority over human beings. Now property became emancipated, as it were; it became the basis for possessive individualism. Thus it mirrored a change in social ethics. The idea of purpose had been replaced by the idea of mechanism. Natural law was emancipated from its previous tie with the laws of nature; nature, in the words of R. H. Tawney, "had come to connote, not divine ordinance, but human appetites."[22]

Within this incipient emancipation a last element has to be considered. There was an increase in population, attributable to an increase in independent households, to improvement in hygiene, and to the successful fight against the spread of plague. Seen from the viewpoint of Modern Europe, this appears as a prologue to the fundamental changes to come. In the course of the nineteenth century the advances in medical science as well as in the transportation of foodstuffs altered the conditions of life for the whole population. Epidemics were fought even more successfully, and starvation became a rare occurrence in most European countries.

Eventually, with further urbanization and with the breakup of the old corporate groups, the age at marriage and the size of families changed. The nineteenth century was to witness a population explo-

[20] This change has been convincingly analyzed by Jean Meuvret "Les idées économiques en France au 17e siècle," in his *Études d'histoire économique* (Paris, 1971).

[21] C. B. MacPherson, *The Political Theory of Possessive Individualism* (Oxford, 1962). For the concept in former centuries, cf. A. Gurevic, "La notion de propriété pendant le haut moyen age," in *Annales*, vol. 27 (1972), pp. 523–547.

[22] *Religion and the Rise of Capitalism* (London, 1926), ch. III, sect. 3, "The Growth of Individualism," p. 180.

sion, and the former way of living was abandoned. With the appearance of factories, large offices, and enlarged civil service, the former unity of living quarters and place of work came to an end.

Only suggestions of this impending transformation can be found in the eighteenth century. Yet by the end of the century observers were fully aware of a fundamental change. In the *Annual Register*'s review of the state of society in 1800,[23] the writer notes three tendencies of the preceding century: The intercourse of men was more extensive, the progression of knowledge was more rapid, and the discoveries of philosophy were increasingly applied to practical purposes. He spoke of "this happy change," resulting "from the progressive intercourses of men with men, minds with minds, of navigation, commerce, arts, and sciences."

According to Sombart the dominant attitude well into the eighteenth century was opposed to dealing publicly with conditions of marketing. Yet in the foremost commercial dictionary of the late seventeenth century Savary had already made "the secrets of trade" public, though he apologized for such audacity. A similar move toward publicity can be seen in advertising. Postlethwayt, in his *Dictionary of Trade of 1774*, calls advertising "a pretty universal practice . . . however mean and disgraceful it was looked on a few years since." He adds that this mode—a new tool of communication, destined to become a potent weapon of modern business—was already initiated by "the way, by which the very government impart their intentions to the kingdom in general," namely through the *Gazette*, "being nothing more than a kind of public advertiser."

Finally, we have to consider the state, its "modernizing" impact as well as its relations to the traditional corporate order.

The State

Once more the conflicts of the Fronde had witnessed armies assembled by the "grands." Only the last of the regencies, the one after the death of Louis XIV, did not lead to armed uprisings. By

[23] Quoted by Perkin, *Origins*, p. 12.

that time Richelieu's principle had become a reality. Likewise in the Empire after the Thirty Years' War only the territorial princes had the right of levying troops and of maintaining fortresses. In England the same process had been almost completed in the early seventeenth century, as Lawrence Stone has shown.[24] Everywhere the razing of castles, the high cost of artillery, the attraction of court life, and the ensuing domestication of the nobility had its share in this development. The professional training of officers made steady progress throughout the seventeenth century—here the Roman example and the humanist influence can be traced via the Netherlands and Sweden to France and Prussia—and military academies had come into being.[25] By the later seventeenth century well-disciplined standing armies had been organized. Despite the survival of older features, such as the claims of noble families to appointments and the sale of commissions, the armed forces were now under the firm control of the ruler.

The earlier discussion about "the crisis in Europe" in the midseventeenth century[26] centered on the violent clashes caused by the fiscal demands arising from the burden of war. The necessity for each state to maintain itself in the fierce European rivalry was indeed at the center of action and thinking. Thinking was dominated by two concepts, reason of state and sovereignty, of which the one dates back to the Renaissance, the other to the late sixteenth century. Within an emerging system of European states they justified the action of supreme power in the state.

No issue was more influential for the centralization of the emerging state and for the professionalization of its services than foreign policy. To the key terms *reason of state* and *sovereignty* correspond two other key terms for the direction of foreign policy, *the European system of states* and *balance of power,* which made their appearance in the late seventeenth century. Simultaneously, *Christendom* was now definitely replaced by *Europe.* Common efforts of Christendom,

[24] Lawrence Stone, *The Crisis of the Aristocracy* (Oxford, 1967), pt. I, ch. V, "Power."

[25] Cf. pp. 90 ff., including nn. 48, 49, this volume. These new features are related to the growth of courts and the resulting domestication of the nobility.

[26] Cf. pp. 94–95, n. 62, this volume.

especially against the Turks, were still envisaged and sometimes even practiced until late in the seventeenth century, and a thinker like Leibniz combined practical political advice with an ecumenical Christian goal. The place of shattered Christian unity was taken by nascent international law, which regularized relations between states; often the system of European states has been called a secularized Corpus Christianum.

Within this system the connection between states became closer, and individual statesmen were aware of it. The Congress of Westphalia at the end of the Thirty Years' War (1648) was the first one in which numerous European states participated to redraw the map of Europe. Such congresses took place well into the eighteenth century and beyond it. This system of European states could accept newcomers as members such as the Russia of Peter the Great. The diplomatic service was regularized; embassies became permanent.

The rational approach within a common civilization now became the recognized basis for the relations between states. The concept of balance of power provided measure and limits for foreign policy. Eventually it extended also into maritime affairs and into the policy of European states in the colonial world. The traditional tendencies of the dynastic state in foreign policy were by no means dead, as shown by the Wars of Succession, which reach into the eighteenth century. Louis XIV took legal claims very seriously, but in the end they were subordinated to balance of power. Frederick the Great's attitude was different. Only after he had entered the Austrian War of Succession did he order his minister to dig out and publicize pertinent territorial claims; his enemy, Maria Theresa, fought him with the conviction of defending her patrimony and her people.

The main emphasis in the analysis of the political institutions of this period had been put on the advance of the so-called absolute government toward efficiency and centralization. It is time to examine this issue, and to ask how much of an advancement actually occurred.

Nowhere did the absolute government abolish elements of the old social–political structure, not even in Denmark, where a special fundamental law proclaimed the exclusive right of the crown to legislate and to appoint, to levy troops and to tax.[27] It operated within the given traditional framework. The rational outlook and the statistical appraisal of resources were particularly at work at the center, but these impulses did not lead to a fundamental reform of the central administration. Even where such an attempt was made as in Prussia, the topical arrangement remained combined with duties of supervision of special regions. In finances the utmost that could be accomplished was an estimate of income and expenses as a tentative basis for a budget. In fact, such a system of accounting in public services, as distinct from double-entry bookkeeping in cost accounting, has been known in Germany from the time of its origin as *cameralist*. In many countries a considerable amount of the revenue was spent locally, and only the surplus was at the disposal of the central administration. The farming out of taxes to financial entrepreneurs remained an accepted device of government. Moreover, on the local level the collecting of taxes—for instance, the taille in France—remained in the hands of locally elected or locally nominated authorities within the population.[28]

Nevertheless, the greatest progress was made in the tightening of control and in the extension of the activities of the agents of the central government. Tocqueville may have overestimated the actual impact of the intendants and underestimated the remaining potentialities of local and regional authorities. Yet intendants and commissioners do indeed mark a new departure. Otto Hintze defines them as "instruments of the new idea of state, unconditionally loyal to the prince, commissioned by him and dependent on him, no longer an officier, but a fonctionnaire."[29] Removable and successively stationed in different areas, they were connected with the region only through their executive subordinates. Originating as agents of the crown to provide for the maintenance of the armed forces, they came into their own in this period, without any limits to

[27] D. Gerhard, "Problème des daenischen Fruehabsolutismus," in *Gesammelte Aufsaetze* (Gottingen, 1977).

[28] Cf. Jean Villain, *Le recouvrement des impôts directs sous l'ancien régime* (Paris, 1952), pp. 22 ff.

[29] "Der Commissarius und seine Bedeutung in der Allgemeinen Geschichte," in *Gesammelte Abhandlungen*, vol. I (1962).

their activity, except for the resistance of the competing traditional forces, such as estates, regional legal–administrative institutions like the French *parlements*, privileged municipalities, estate owners with feudal claims, peasant communes, and so on.

Through the whole of the previous period functions had been ill defined. Any office to which someone was appointed by the crown had been regarded less as an administrative function than as a source of social prestige and income. Loyseau, the main theorist of offices, explained the office in 1610 as "irremovable dignity with public function." The new state servant of the eighteenth century—the intendant or commissioner—was even less circumscribed in his functions, but the functions were the raison d'être of his position. His foremost concern were the armed forces, which meant that he had to keep his area "taxable." It was his duty to maintain and to develop its resources. By way of a newly developing administrative law he encroached on the sphere of older legal–administrative institutions, such as the *parlements* in France or the *Regierungen* in Prussia, taking as his guide not customary and positive law but the needs of the state.

Even in the early seventeenth century cases of a fiscal nature had been withdrawn from the regular jurisdiction and had been handled by governmental agencies, such as in France the Conseil d'Etat, or on a lower level the Cours des Aides. Now such problems became the concern of the intendants. In this way the central government tried to overcome what the greatest expert on the history of taxation, Gabriel Ardant, in his analysis of the preceding centuries has called *la résistance du milieu*, the established customs and the opposition of local and regional authorities of Old Europe.[30]

Yet even these new servants of the crown, the commissioners and intendants, can by no means be equated with modern civil servants. Like other officeholders—unless these had bought their office—they had no security of tenure. Only in the course of the eighteenth century did their appointment extend beyond a few years and eventually even beyond the reign of an individual prince; only then was the attachment to a ruler replaced by service to the state. Moreover,

[30] Gabriel Ardant, *L'histoire de l'impôt* (Paris, 1971); cf. also Ardant's contribution to Charles Tilly, ed., *The Formation of National States in Western Europe* (Princeton, 1975).

the salary was insufficient. To a large extent it had to be supplemented by the holding of several offices and by fees.

The contribution of the intendants to the strengthening of the central government has been thoroughly investigated.[31] Not till the eighteenth century did their offices become fully established.[32] By that time they tended to stay longer in a specific region, and their local connections became stronger. It has been said that they became "in a sense . . . a half-way house between the commissioner and the office-holder."[33] They depended a great deal on *subdélégués,* local officials who had bought offices. According to Sagnac, anyone who was charged with supervising the *officiers* had to take recourse to *officiers* in order to control a region.[34] The intendants were trained by way of the expensive corporation of the *maîtres des requêtes.* Thus early in their careers they were already more or less associated with families of the *parlements,* or they were taken from them. And when the commissioners were more independent, as they were in Prussia, they had frequently to cope with the opposition of the old judicial–administrative bodies, the Prussian *Regierungen.*[35]

Eventually (and in this area Prussia and Austria led the way) cameralist (i.e., economic) knowledge was required in addition to or instead of the customary legal training. Entrance examinations conducted by the government began in the later eighteenth century. By screening possible candidates the central government gradually became independent of the corporate groups of lawyers and officeholders. Thus the way was opened for a government career in the modern professional sense, though patronage and sale of offices did not become extinct. In England a civil service did not emerge prior to the middle of the nineteenth century.

The nascent modern state was often supported by national feel-

[31] Last analysis in Richard Bonney, *Political Change in France under Richelieu and Mazarin* (Oxford, 1978).

[32] Cf. the articles of J. Ricommand in *Revue d'histoire moderne,* vol. 12(1937), and in *Revue historique de droit français* (1942).

[33] Bonney, *Political Change,* p. 451.

[34] Ph. Sagnac, *La formation de la société française moderne,* vol. I (Paris, 1945), p. 62.

[35] Otto Hintze, "Preussens Entwicklung zum Rechtsstaat," in *Gesammelte Abhandlungen,* vol. III (1962).

ing. As literacy and literary production increased, the national institutions of crown and parliament could count on an ever-widening
public beyond the age-old attachment of lawyers. Significantly,
scholars in their publications turned ever more from Latin to the
vernacular. The state itself—the crown and in some countries
parliament—offered the focal point for national consciousness. A
national state became its own justification. At the end of the eighteenth century the partitions of Poland—itself a multinational
state—destroyed in the name of the balance of power the independence of the Polish nation; many contemporaries regarded
these partitions as a crime.

When in the early seventeenth century the legislative initiative
had been won by the English parliament, the foundation had been
laid for a new active role of a representative assembly. After the
great revolutionary upheaval of the seventeenth century had been
overcome, a "political nation," as J. H. Plumb has called it,[36] had
emerged. On the Continent the officialdom of the absolute state accomplished at least a greater cohesion by appealing to the population at large. By the late seventeenth century the term *country*
denoted above all the whole of England, only rarely an individual
county. In the Continental countries the term *nation* passed through
a similar process. Let us be cautious, however, not to overestimate
these tendencies. According to Otto Hintze, as late as the middle of
the eighteenth century regional authorities within the Prussian
monarchy regarded every area outside of their region as "abroad,"
whether it belonged to Prussia or to the empire or to another European state.[37] Terms like *nation provençale, nation bretonne,* or *nation
franc-comtoise* were still current on the eve of the French
Revolution.[38]

It remains to appraise the relative strength and resistance of corporate and regional forces in order to present a true picture of this
period.

[36] J. H. Plumb, *The Growth of Political Stability in England 1675–1725* (London,
1967).
[37] "Behoerdenorganisation und allgemeine Verwaltung in Preussen um 1740,"
in *Acta Borussica,* vol. VI, no.1 (1901), p. 81.
[38] P. Ardacheff, *Les intendants de province sous Louis XVI* (Paris, 1909), ch. II; cf.
also Chr. Mueller, *Das Imperative und das Freie Mandat* (Leiden, 1966).

Weakening and Persistence of the Corporate Order

The corporate order had never embraced the entire population. With the growth of large cities, especially the capital cities, the peripheral elements, the poor (i.e., the dependent), had increased. In the countryside the fragmentation of peasants' lots had augmented the segment of the cottagers who were not full members of the village commune.[39] In areas close to cities they had been integrated as laborers into the putting-out system. As previously indicated,[40] they had been recurrently involved in revolts; they had never organized as a group. Though their numbers grew with the upswing of the economy, they still lacked strength and the will to act as an independent group. They did not challenge the traditional structure, in program or in action. This is also true for the increasing number of villagers not in the neighborhood of cities who were employed at home by merchant–entrepreneurs in textile and other manufacturing and who had been unable to support themselves through agriculture since the seventeenth century. They were the precursors of the workers employed in the domestic industry of the nineteenth century.

Their condition was often extremely miserable, and many scholars have regarded them as part of the modern industrial proletariat. Yet their external living conditions and their outlook were quite different from those of industrial workers. They lived in the village, even when they no longer participated in communal property and rights. As a result their working time was irregular; it was related to ecclesiastical and village traditions. Here time had not yet been incorporated into the elements of a market economy.[41]

It was change within the upper levels of society that undermined the corporate order. The upswing in the economy noticeable in most European countries since the 1730s has not yet been sufficiently investigated, especially its consequences. It can be asserted

[39] Cf. pp. 67 ff., this volume.

[40] Cf. p. 69, including n. 17, this volume.

[41] Cf. the contemporary observations quoted by Medick in P. Kriedte, H. Medick, and J. Schlumbohm, *Industrialisierung vor der Industrialisierung* (Gottingen, 1977), pp. 138 ff.

that mobile capital grew in strength and that merchants and entrepreneurs became more numerous. Simultaneously the enlargement of a "public" and the growth of governmental services created a large number of "intellectuals"—authors without institutional ties—and officeholders who had no place within the corporate structure. Formerly, merchants and officials had found a niche within that rather elastic framework through ennoblement and landholding, though not without opposition from the ranks of those they wanted to join. Now the sheer weight of numbers worked against absorption; legal devices for retaining the land in the hands of noble families such as "strict settlement" in England or entail on the Continent, increasingly common since the seventeenth century, reduced the amount of landed estates available for newcomers. *Standspersoner* in Sweden and *Briefadel* in Germany became a problem; officials, whether ennobled or not, had no definite place in the corporate order.[42]

The attitude of the crown toward the corporate order was ambiguous. Kings and princes regarded themselves as standing at the head of a pyramid stemming from feudal times. Even Frederick the Great, who wrote with utmost sarcasm about princes, considered the bond between himself and his nobility the greatest resource of the state. Nobles remained the mainstay of the armed services on which the strength of states was built. Since the seventeenth century, military service and court life had disciplined the nobles.

For centuries the princes had accepted and perfected ranks and honors, and new titles of nobility had been added. Thus the traditional hierarchical order had been strengthened, with the aim of integrating the corporate structure more closely into the state. On the other hand, many old privileges lost their meaning when the government assumed the functions of lords and municipalities. In some countries, such as England or Prussia, local government by the nobility continued under the supervision of the state. In many regions of France seigneurs had become estranged from their dependents, and the latter felt the burden of their obligations all the more heavily. In the words of Tocqueville, the French feudality had

---

[42] Sten Carlsson, *Ståondsamhaelle och Ståondspersoner 1700–1865* (Lund, 1949); K. S. Bader, "Zur Lage und Haltung des schwaebischen Adels am Ende des Alten Reiches," in *Zeitschrift fuer Wuerttembergische Landesgeschichte*, vol. 5 (1941).

remained the greatest of all "civil" (i.e., social) institutions while ceasing to be a political institution.[43]

Contrary to an often expressed opinion, the so-called absolute ruler, while establishing his institutions alongside the old corporate order, very rarely, and only by "necessity" claimed the right of the reversibility of privileges. "We must be aware of the time when agreements were concluded; what in a bygone past may have been appropriate does not suffice in present times"—this statement of a Wuerttemberg prince in 1738 is the argument of a new era.[44]

The absolute state would not and could not abolish the autonomous intermediate bodies. They were instrumental in the levying of taxes for which in France the local community was jointly responsible, and which in Prussia the regional nobility collected from the peasantry. New immigrants like the reformed refugees from Louis XIV were organized in Prussia as autonomous colonies.

The traditional authorities succeeded in temporarily resisting attempts to establish a unified code for the whole state or to equalize the status of its subjects. In the discussion of kingship in the period of the crystallization of Old Europe, the reader was cautioned not to overrate the success of endeavors for territorial control.[45] As late as 1688 an Austrian author demanded that strict attention should be paid to the status (*Stand und Qualität*) of each person so that he or she might be properly indicted by the pertinent authority ("damit ein jeder von seiner Obrigkeit competenter beklagt werde"). A contemporary Austrian scholar regards as the decisive reform enacted by Maria Theresa the organization of the state in terms of the territory, no longer in terms of the different varieties of personal status ("nicht nach dem Personal-, sondern nach dem Flaechenprinzip").[46]

The rulers proceeded cautiously. The old coexistence of authorities was becoming more difficult as the concept of sover-

---

[43] *L'ancien régime et la révolution*, at the end of ch. I of bk. II.

[44] W. Grube, *Der Stuttgarter Landtag* (Stuttgart, 1957), p. 396.

[45] Cf. ch. 3, pp. 52 ff., this volume.

[46] Nicolaus von Beckmann, *Idea iuris statutarii et consuetudinarii Stiriaci et Austriaci* (1688), p. 218; Alfred Hoffmann, "Die Quellen zur Geschichte der Wirtschaft im Lande ob der Enns," in *Mitteilungen des Oberoesterreichischen Landesarchivs,* vol. I (Linz, 1950), p. 113.

eignty, postulating a place of final decision, made headway. To be sure, in former centuries frictions between crown and estates, between different estates, and within individual estates, had not been lacking. With the reception of Roman law the concept of a highest authority had gained in precision. Now, because of the theory of sovereignty, a divisive influence came into existence. During the seventeenth century, for instance, in German imperial cities the organized citizenry—itself a limited corporate group—protested that they were not "subjects" of the magistrate, and questioned the magistrate's right of supreme power.[47]

Eventually uniformity and full control over all subjects became the goal of the "enlightened absolutism" of the rulers of the late eighteenth century. The numbering of houses in France and Austria, introduced for purposes of conscription, was indicative of the change that the actions of governments implied. In 1785 a Swiss patrician regarded the numbering of houses in neighboring Austrian territories as "symbolic of the hand of the ruler stretching out inexorably over the individual house."[48]

In the internal struggles of the seventeenth century the monopoly of power had been acquired by the state. As a consequence many cities were dismantled, and others later lost their walls in a process that continued far into the nineteenth century. Militarily, and often economically, as a result of the endeavors of the state to create larger fiscal units, cities no longer had to fulfill their old functions. Yet both cities and regions were reluctant to cooperate in the wider unity of state and nation. Characteristically the most violent conflict of the French crown with regional forces and eventually with the whole body of the *parlements,* the *affaire de Bretagne* of the 1760s, centered on the building and maintenance of roads.[49] As part of a newly established great network of arteries of transportation for the

[47] Otto Brunner, "Souveraenitaetsproblem und Sozialstruktur in den deutschen Reichsstaedten der Fruehen Neuzeit," in *Neue Wege der Verfassungs- und Sozialgeschichte,* 2nd ed. (Gottingen, 1968).

[48] Ludwig Meyer von Knonau, quoted by R. Feller, "Von der alten Eidgenossenschaft," in *Schweizerische Akademiereden,* ed. F. Strich (Bern, 1945), p. 458.

[49] R. R. Palmer, *The Age of Democratic Revolution,* vol. I (Princeton, 1959), ch. IV, p. 93.

whole state, road building became an affair of the central government, requiring the forced labor previously demanded only for
regional purposes.

Of the tendencies that threatened multiformity, hierarchy,
regionalism, and rank, none were more powerful than the ideas that
had led to the Enlightenment, and which the Enlightenment
elaborated. These were the ideas of social contract, natural law—no
longer associated with Christian divine law—and natural rights.
They protected the individual from transgressions by government;
they included the right to property—property no longer combined
with a function of authority.

This development paralleled the change in basic philosophical
cosmological concepts owing to the Scientific Revolution. The inherently hierarchical cosmology of the spheres had been accepted
for centuries without questioning. It had now been challenged and
rejected.[50] The acceptance of rank and order had mirrored traditional cosmology. Hence the intermediate authorities between
prince and people now had to establish their own rational defense.

R. R. Palmer has shown that "conservatism and counter revolution were not mere reactions against revolutions, but eighteenth
century forces against which revolution itself was a reaction."[51]
These "constituted bodies"—to quote Palmer—claimed that they
(i.e., the established corporate authorities, such as assemblies of
estates, judicial–administrative courts like the French *parlements,*
and municipal councils) had a power of their own. According to
them their power was not based on delegation by the people; the
families from which their members were recruited had a special
ability and right of government.

Bolstering institutions by an appeal to history had been an old
device to justify their position, frequently not without deliberate
distortion of facts. A general theory of intermediate powers had to
wait until the eighteenth century, when Montesquieu acted as a
kind of godfather. Heretofore the aristocratic society and the hierar-

[50] Cf. pp. 114 ff., this volume.
[51] Palmer, *Age of Democratic Revolution,* at the end of ch. I.

chy of ranks had rarely been questioned; now they had to be defended against a new world view.

The concept of representation changed. In the past representation had meant delegation of power by those who in their sphere held authority; it had not required specific justification. In the eighteenth century the organization of assemblies of estates was often justified functionally as composed of the three estates of society. Representation referred increasingly to a larger constituency. It envisaged an electorate, although previously an electorate had rarely been taken into consideration. At the end of the period the movement for parliamentary reform, for an enlargement of the electorate, started in Britain.

When the old social–political structure dissolved and authority was increasingly monopolized by a central government, "society" emerged as an independent force, its advance matching the advance of the state. Society was closely associated with the appearance of the "public," and with concern for publicity.

In times of storm and stress, in periods of attack on the supreme power, as early as the seventeenth century political writers had reached out to a larger public. In France the countless *mazarinades* of the Fronde were indicative of the broadening of the political appeal. The pamphlet literature of the English Revolution had by far transcended even these dimensions. The influence of puritanism, leading also to greater literacy, had its share in the enlargement of the public. The violent conflict opened parliamentary proceedings also; in numerous ways they had often been communicated to the nation, though never officially.

In the eighteenth century—for Great Britain a period of stability and prosperity—the assemblies of estates increasingly began to look outward. Both in England and in Sweden the public was informed in different ways of their proceedings. The assemblies grew to be more representative in the new sense. Taking the place of the old corporate ties, national parties began to be formed. In the end the national idea and the national state, more than any other idea and any other power, were to dominate the modern epoch.

In the writings of Scottish philosopher–sociologists investigations of human relations as a whole appeared. Soon society was to be contrasted with state and government. The old entity—what in this book has been called the social–political structure—was dissolved.

Independently of the old corporate and regional structure a new type of affiliation developed in the eighteenth century, the voluntary association. The freely formed religious denominations of the sixteenth and seventeenth centuries may be considered their forerunners.[52] Now voluntary associations with specific social or political aims began to flourish, especially in England, tied neither to locality, region, nor corporate group. In some way political parties can be regarded as a type of voluntary association.

All these new formations were offspring of a new individualistic age that ever more consciously fought for emancipation, believing in progress. The change in outlook was mirrored in the new meaning of the word *revolution*.[53] The term had been part of a cosmic world view. The concept of the revolving of the celestial bodies was then adopted for human history. The English, as late as 1688, coined the term *glorious revolution,* when after half a century of violent conflict and upheaval their history seemed to have reverted to a happy balance of crown and parliament, which was interpreted as a restitution of the old relationship. Yet at the same time the word began to be used for basic changes, especially, though not only, of a political nature. By the late eighteenth century the term had acquired a new meaning: a break with the past, a violent turn toward a better future. The modern, revolutionary age began with the French Revolution. About a century later a historian called the turn toward the Machine Age in Great Britain, which was coeval with the French Revolution, the Industrial Revolution.[54]

---

[52] Cf. pp. 105 ff., including n. 81, this volume.

[53] This problem was first discussed by Eugen Rosenstock Huessy, *Out of Revolution* (New York, 1938), in the chapter on England, and by Karl Griewank, *Der neuzeitliche Revolutionsbegriff* (Weimar, 1955); cf. also Vernon F. Snow, "The Concept of Revolution in Seventeenth Century England," in *Historical Journal*, vol. 56 (1962).

[54] Arnold Toynbee, *Lectures on the Industrial Revolution of the Eighteenth Century in England* (London 1884; reprinted New York, 1960).

The complete break with the past became apparent in the early stages of the French Revolution, not prior to it. To the very end of the *Ancien Régime* the new forces had not waged a frontal assault on the old order. Only in the last months prior to assembling the French Estates General did the old mode of assembling them in the traditional corporate order begin to be questioned. One of the best experts for the history of this period, George V. Taylor, has stated, "The intention to smash the legal basis of nobility, and, along with it, the whole system of language, symbols, images, and formalities that reinforced the subservience of the lower groups, was a product of the revolutionary crisis, not a cause."[55] Yet even several years after the famous night of August 4, 1789, the Prussian *Allgemeine Landrecht* retained a society organized in estates as its basis, though functionally integrated into the state, adding officialdom as another corporate order.[56] Old Europe indeed died slowly. Some elements of the former structure had to be incorporated into a society with the dominant urge for democracy and equality. In this new era the place of "liberties"—the privileges—was taken by the postulate of liberty for each individual.

[55] George V. Taylor, "Noncapitalist Wealth and the Origins of the French Revolution," in *American Historical Review*, vol. 72 (1967), p. 493; Eberhard Schmitt, *Repraesentation und Revolution* (Munich, 1969).

[56] See the discussion of the *Landrecht* and of its functional appraisal of estates in Mack Walker, "Rights and Functions: The Social Categories of Eighteenth Century German Jurists and Cameralists," in *Journal of Modern History*, vol. 50 (1978).

6

Epilogue: Looking Beyond

Individual liberty and equality, whether conceived as separate goals or, more frequently, in combination, were never lost sight of from this point on. They remained a battle cry of the movements that continued or recurrently revived the dynamic impulse of the French Revolution. Fundamentally, and on principle, they were opposed to the remnants of the corporate order of Old Europe. Yet history does not know of any complete break. The fact of the survival of corporate traits throughout a period of revolutionary changes is ample proof of how deeply they had been ingrained in the structure of Old Europe.

The social–political earthquake that shook Europe from 1789 to 1815 had no precedent in the convulsions of former centuries. Napoleon had brought about a temporary end to these revolutionary changes, though he had been both their catalyst and their moderator.

The power of the upheaval is apparent from the political map of Europe. Independent city-republics, both in the Mediterranean area and in central Europe—the oldest amongst them, Venice, almost antedated the formation of Europe—political control by knightly orders and by ecclesiastical authorities, small feudal principalities, the Holy Roman Empire of the German nation—they all disappeared. All of them had been characteristic forms of Old Europe.

In France the creation of departments in an early phase of the Revolution marked the turn away from regional attachment. It found its consummation in Napoleon's system of centrally appointed prefects. And though for him popular sovereignty served rather as a pretense, in several cases of territorial changes he continued the Revolutionary use of plebiscites in a perverted form—a measure that would have been inconceivable in the preceding centuries of dynastic claims and of wars of succession.

Internally a uniform legislation established equality before the law. The introduction or adoption of the Code Napoleon secured this fundamental change in large areas of Europe. In other parts, as in Prussia, reform legislation matched in some degree the accomplishments of Napoleonic control. By the middle of the nineteenth century—in some areas under the impact of the revolutionary eruption of 1848—the dominant urge for emancipation had established an equal footing for all different groups of society. The repeal of political disabilities of religious minorities, the emancipation of the Jews, the emancipation of the peasants, the abolition of craft guilds, the opening up of trade—all these changes and many related steps are different phases of one great process that was initiated by the French Revolution.

In the end, though not without further struggle, the uniform state replaced the corporate structure. In the increasingly mobile society classes tended to take the place of the former estates. In the period of the French Revolution, after the destruction of the corporate order, the term *classes* appeared for the first time in the specific modern sense; it immediately had the connotation of class conflict. The bourgeois historians of the early nineteenth century, François

Guizot and Augustin Thierry, already used the term for the interpretation of the past, as Marx and Engels later did, too.

Nevertheless, though the old structure of Europe had been shattered, some of its main components survived for a long time, more
or less successfully adjusting themselves to the new situation.

In Britain, the country of gradual reform, eventually the model of
parliamentary democracy, the crown abandoned any influence on
the formation of government in the course of the nineteenth century. Simultaneously suffrage was broadened and voting became
secret. Yet the old aristocracy, strengthened, as formerly, by newly
assimilated members, retained a place even within the elected
chamber.

In central Europe, especially in Prussia, monarchy and landed
aristocracy remained entrenched in a different way. Here the king
continued as an independent power to face elected parliaments,
since the middle of the nineteenth century within the limits set by a
constitution. Here the nobility eventually became allied with a reformed and reforming civil service, the descendant of eighteenth-
century enlightened absolutism.

In both countries, in Britain as well as in Prussia, educational
reforms gave a new vindication to the formation of an elite that
would also encompass the traditional governing groups. The
gentleman, or the *Gebildete,* an individual to be formed after a
classical model, was the ideal to which education, at least in theory
and institutional adaptation, aspired in the respective countries.

When King Maximilian of Bavaria asked Ranke in 1854 which
tendencies of their own century he regarded as predominant, Ranke
included the confrontation of monarchy and popular sovereignty.[1]
In Old Europe the crown had indeed been the focal point for the
political consciousness of the emerging nations; it was the crown
that had helped them into existence. Of all the emancipations that
were initiated by the French Revolution, none was more fundamental than what may be called the emancipation of the nations. Na-

---

[1] Leopold von Ranke, *Ueber die Epochen der Neueren Geschichte.* Nineteenth Lecture, last section.

tional feeling surpassed religious attachment. As it were, it often became the religion of the nineteenth century. Wherever loyalty to the crown still existed and wherever it was taught, it was submerged in national feeling. Since the French Revolution, the nation was anchored in the democratic concept of popular sovereignty.

In France the July Revolution of 1830 put an end to any attempt to return to the old order. None of the later experimental changes of government aimed at a restoration of the past. The far-reaching significance of the events of 1830 was already fully recognized by two of the most influential historians and most independent observers of the contemporary scene, Barthold Georg Niebuhr and Alexis de Tocqueville.

Niebuhr had belonged to the circle of the Prussian reformers; their achievements were in line with the early principles of the French Revolution. Yet throughout his life Niebuhr remained in unremitting opposition to the radical egalitarian movement that originated from the later phase of the Revolution. To him the events of July 1830 indicated not just another outbreak of the revolutionary fever; they rather showed that the revolutionary movement, far from having been channeled into beneficial reforms, was an ongoing process that was about to destroy European culture. In fear of a complete break with the European tradition, he died in sorrow and despair a few months later.

To Tocqueville, 25 years old, a generation younger than Niebuhr, the events of 1830 gave direction to his political thought. It was shaped by constant observation of the contemporary social and political scene and by intense study of the new American democracy, a study for which the July Revolution had provided the incentive. From now on all his writings were influenced by the appraisal of his own times, of whose dynamic, revolutionary implications he was convinced. He saw this development as a conflict between two ideas, the idea of political liberty and the quasi-providential urge for equality. The latter, moving beyond equality before the law toward the demand for equality of conditions, in his opinion endangered political liberty; yet for him attainment of political liberty was the most essential task, in place of the liberties—the privileges—of a bygone aristocratic age.

In an early phase of the radical revolutionary movement, prior to Marx, Saint-Simon and Proudhon had operated with the concept of the Revolution as an ongoing process.[2] At the beginning of the next century Trotsky coined the term Permanent Revolution as a maxim and to denominate his and future times—the counterpole to what in this book has been described as Old Europe. Thirty years earlier Jacob Burckhardt had lectured on the Age of the French Revolution. He stated that the whole period since was indeed an Age of Revolution, and that this "great drama" was likely to be more and more in contrast to the whole known past of the planet.[3]

By the beginning of the twentieth century the paramount political force was the national state, which had developed out of the dynastic state. It showed its strength at the outbreak of World War I when even most of the socialists rallied around the national banner. As early as the Revolution of 1848 the national feeling had prevailed, when independent action by national minorities in the multinational dynastic states hindered the formation of a common front of the popular forces. Since that time, the composite states, as they had been inherited from Old Europe, had come under increasing attack by the minorities. In this age of nationalism the old consciousness of a common European heritage deteriorated, though it remained stronger with the governments than with the population.

By the end of the nineteenth century governments had to satisfy an ever larger community. They depended on, or at least had to cooperate with, parliaments that were elected by ballot on the basis of universal suffrage. The parliaments had moved far away from the limited constituencies of the assemblies of estates of Old Europe, which had been largely based on privilege. Hence political parties, too, had outgrown their early nineteenth-century phase of assemblies of notables encompassing a small, politically educated

---

[2] Theodor Schieder, "Das Problem der Revolution im 19. Jahrhundert," in *Staat und Gesellschaft im Wandel unserer Zeit* (Munich, 1958).

[3] "Das Revolutionszeitalter," in *Historische Fragmente,* ed. E. Duerr and W. Kaegi (Stuttgart, 1957), especially p. 269 (November 6, 1871).

electorate. They had to cater to the whole population, most of all to special and vociferous economic interests.

In line with the idea of popular sovereignty, general education had eliminated illiteracy and had created the basis for general political participation. Technological advance kept pace with this change; the enlargement of the public was matched by the increasing impact of the press. At the end of 1830 Niebuhr kept himself informed about the further impact of the July Revolution by reading the papers at his club; thus he contracted the pneumonia that caused his death. Thirty years later the rotary printing press made large-scale publication and circulation of inexpensive newspapers possible.

At the same time "the population explosion" of Modern Europe continued. By 1900 the number of its inhabitants since 1700 had roughly quadrupled. Further improvement of hygiene contributed to the increase, and the progress of medical science cut the mortality rate, especially of infants. Simultaneously modern industry and the fundamental change in transportation through railways created living conditions totally different from those of Old Europe. In addition, once the corporate structure had been abolished, restrictions on founding a family had disappeared and the age at marriage had become lower.

Historians call the economic and technological development initiated in England in the late eighteenth century the *Industrial Revolution,* a term coined by an English historian about 100 years later.[4] By that time this continuing process had reached most countries of the Continent. None of the contemporary observers presented its worldwide implications, the inexorable advance of mobile capital and its no less inexorable revolutionizing impact on human relations, with more vigor than did Karl Marx. It is neither possible nor necessary within the context of this epilogue to analyze the fundamental change involved in this process. It may be sufficient to remind the reader that economic and political developments were inextricably intertwined. The growth of modern business, of industry and technology, and the growth of the modern state conditioned each other. Max Weber has pointed out that the rational spirit was the specific characteristic of Western civilization; it became domi-

[4] Cf. p. 136, n. 54, this volume.

nant only now. Rational organization and procedure, demanding strict work discipline, prevailed, and the formation of a bureaucracy paralleled the all-permeating influence of modern business. The state was no longer hemmed in by the former restrictions of regionalism and corporatism. It had to cope with, or to accept, the impact of social and economic forces competing at large.

Under these conditions the family as a working unit was dissolved. It persisted only in exceptional cases. Centralized enterprises and offices became the rule not only in industry and commerce, but also in government service—in the latter case essentially beginning in the eighteenth century; eventually this happened even in the professions. The place of work with its strict daily requirement replaced the old entity of family and work, which survived longest in agriculture. The psychological impact of this fundamental change can hardly be appraised.

Against this background the individual in the modern democratic society has to be seen. Perhaps nobody has interpreted the impending change and its implications more discerningly than Tocqueville. In the 1830s he contrasted the coming modern society and the past "aristocratic" (i.e., corporate) age. In a discussion of *individualism* (a term brought into circulation by Tocqueville) in democratic countries, he stated that in aristocratic ages and nations all generations become, as it were, contemporaneous, and a man knows and respects his forefathers and thinks of his remote descendants as if they were already present; in democratic countries the human bond is extended, but relaxed, and here the individuals acquire the habit of considering themselves as always standing alone.[5]

A few years later Karl Marx, in his analysis of Hegel's concept of alienation as the process of man's consciousness in history, began to focus on the estrangement of the wage earner from the product of his work. It was the starting point for his criticism of capitalism, which later found its expression in *Das Kapital*. These "Parisian" economic–philosophical manuscripts of Marx[6] were not discovered until the 1930s, about 100 years after Tocqueville's observations.

[5] *De la démocratie en Amérique* (first published in 1840), pt. II, sect. II, ch. II.

[6] Karl Marx, *Fruehe Schriften,* vol. I (Stuttgart, 1962), ed. Lieber; *Philosophische Manuskripte* (1948), pp. 506–665.

Together with the findings of psychoanalysis, the reinterpretation of Marx endowed the sociological concept of "alienation" with a central meaning for the analysis of the changing world of the mid-twentieth century.

By that time Europe had completely broken away from its original corporate basis. Now even the oldest of the estates, the priesthood, whose independence, attained by the Reform Papacy, had facilitated the crystallization of the other estates, is being challenged in its unique position by recent developments in the Catholic Church.

At the beginning of the twentieth century Werner Sombart attempted to analyze the main features of the modern capitalistic development. He presented the new phase of man's material existence as breaking away from the limited resources of previous centuries. He emphatically pointed out that a new age had come into existence when "Western man" (to use our contemporary terminology) for the first time turned on a large scale from the use of organic nature to the deliberate exploitation of inorganic nature and to the discovery of new sources of energy. Earlier, Jacob Burckhardt had called the preceding epoch—the period of Old Europe—"an age of helpful retardation," adding: "If they had exploited the earth as much as we do, most likely we would not exist."[7] It was not until our own times that the consequences of this fundamental change were envisaged by an increasing number of our contemporaries.

Not least as a result of economic necessities, Europe had turned toward the outside world by the late nineteenth century. Historians usually refer to the period prior to World War I as the Age of Imperialism. Nevertheless, until about 1930 the history of Europe could still be seen as an entity in itself. In this period older traditions persisted amidst an increasingly industrialized democratic society. Most of all, its self-confidence had not yet been shaken. A universal mind like Max Weber's had analyzed underlying religious concepts

[7] *Historische Fragmente,* introductory section, "Neuere Geschichte von 1450 bis 1598."

of non-Western civilizations, though originally not for their own sake. His purpose had been to establish the premises for the uniqueness of the West, for its victory over other civilizations.

Undoubtedly, since the turn of the century a malaise about the achievements of the age began to be felt. Antirationalist writers questioned even the unique significance of European civilization. The negative appraisal of Europe's position within the contemporary world found its expression in historical–philosophical writings, such as Oswald Spengler's *Decline of the West.* It took the events of the mid-twentieth century, leading to what has been called "the political collapse of Europe,"[8] to destroy European self-centeredness. After the destruction of two world wars Europe had to find its place in the face of the rivalry of the superpowers.

Some scholars are inclined to talk of our own times as of "the post-modern age." The steep advance of emancipated science and technology are its main characteristics, with the accompanying host of almost insoluble problems of modernization, or rather, Westernization. An ever-accelerating pace and ubiquity are the outstanding traits of the present age—the acceleration of the historical process and the ability and inclination to develop productive forces without restraint by nature or space. In a society that has to adapt to continuous change, in an age of discontinuity, the survival of the "scientific–technological world" has become a main concern,[9] to be investigated in its basic premises. It may well be that a new age has begun.

---

[8] Hajo Holborn, *The Political Collapse of Europe* (New York, 1951).

[9] One of the institutes of the Max-Planck-Gesellschaft is called *Institut zur Erforschung der Lebensbedingungen der wissenschaftlich-technischen Welt* (Institute for the investigation of the living conditions of the scientific–technological world).